NANCY L. CLARK

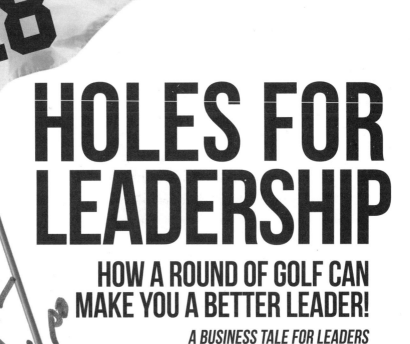

18 HOLES FOR LEADERSHIP

HOW A ROUND OF GOLF CAN MAKE YOU A BETTER LEADER!

A BUSINESS TALE FOR LEADERS

Library of Congress Control Number: 2010936542
ISBN-13: 978-0-615-40605-3

18 Holes for Leadership soft-cover edition 2010
Printed in the United States of America
For more information about special discounts for bulk purchases,
please contact 3L Publishing at 916.300.8012 or log onto our website at
www.3LPublishing.com.
Design by Erin Pace.

Dedicated to my father, John S. Clark, Jr. —
The most compassionate teacher, listener, encourager and
leader I have known.

NANCY L. CLARK

CONTENTS

NANCY L. CLARK

NANCY L. CLARK

INTRODUCTION

I regularly bristle at the typically condescending statements from business people about the "soft stuff." They generally mean the people elements of the business such as talent management, training, coaching, communication, etc. I, too, was once like them. Working in the family business, I earned the nickname, "Little General" by the time I was 12. I was all about facts, equipment, process, technology, etc. – the "hard stuff." The human elements were secondary; "real leaders" didn't worry about the "soft stuff," and they certainly wouldn't pursue a career in human resources or talent management.

I now know that I was all wrong. My realization evolved, but definitely hit home about 20 years ago. As a business systems consultant for Arthur Andersen at the time, I worked with companies to create their technology strategies. Since the technology plan should enable and complement the business goals, I always started with requesting the overall strategic plan. For small- and medium-sized companies (and to my surprise an occasional large company as well), I regularly discovered that no such plan existed. I found myself consequently facilitating leadership teams to develop their overall strategic plans. It became abundantly clear that high-performing leaders and teams were different. The lessons from my father were becoming clear and evident — technology, equipment, processes, etc., were comparatively easy. Getting the right people into the right jobs doing the right things was truly the "hard" stuff.

It became strikingly obvious that every business is a *people* business. Take away the people, and you have no business. World-class leaders understand that, others do not.

Now with more years of experience than I care to admit, I continue to be a student of leadership, human behavior and performance. Working with hundreds of companies, teams and leaders, I dedicate my time transferring knowledge, applying analytics, coaching leaders, and aligning resources. My stated mission for years has been to *help companies be healthy, profitable, and great places for people to work*. The good news is that these elements are not mutually exclusive; you can have it all. The key is leadership. Ultimately leadership is about creating a culture, leading change, and driving performance. However, those things are results of what and how you lead. This book is about what it takes to get those results.

With the right leaders, an organization has the greatest possibility of reaching world-class status. I say possibility because so many factors impact the destiny of a company (e.g., economy). However, with the wrong leaders, an organization has virtually no chance of winning for the long term — they may be lucky in the short run, but the long term is doomed.

Combining my experience with my mission to help organizations, I am determined to unpack the mystery of leadership for current and future leaders. It is a complex subject and suggests why organizations have trouble in finding or building leaders who have all or most of the package. I propose that there are two parts to the leadership "equation:"

1. Capability elements: (Do you have what it takes?); and

2. Effectiveness elements. (Do you know what to do with it?)

Rather than offer a dry, academic account, I chose to convey the elements through a story. Masked in a business fable, Samantha (kindly referred to as "Sam") guides us through the leadership equation. A consultant and business coach for many years, Sam is called upon to coach Paul, a high-level executive of one of her clients. Not a golfer herself, she finds herself in the unfortunate position of playing a round of golf with him. Thus, she uses golf to unwrap the leadership elements and to challenge and coach Paul.

In full disclosure, yes, Sam is me. However, all the other characters are fictional. In truth, they are bits and pieces sewn together from many, many leaders I have known, worked with, and/or coached. Their names have been changed to protect the innocent as well as the guilty.

Whether you are the CEO of a billion-dollar company, a sole proprietor, a first-time supervisor, or a parent wanting to offer guidance to your child, I hope you find this book helpful. Whatever the case, my goal is to provide a framework to understand leadership, furnish insights on what to do to improve, and ultimately to help organizations become healthy, profitable and great places for people to do great work.

THE CHALLENGE

NANCY L. CLARK

HOLE-Y MOLE-Y

"Dave, you are not helping!" My husband couldn't stop laughing. "Just help me find my golf shoes. I don't believe this — where are they? Shouldn't they just be in the bag?"

"Remember the last time you played, I took everything out and cleaned it for you. I put them back in your bag." Dave said trying to be helpful.

"Here they are. Thanks honey. If my game isn't polished, at least my golf shoes are. Wish me luck. I may be the only consultant in the world who in one outing successfully destroys both her career and her best network — the country club. Oh well, it's been a great ride. See you tonight. Please have a gin and tonic waiting!"

"I'll make it a double ... bogey that is!"

"Very funny!"

As I drove to the club, I continued to chastise myself for suggesting a round of golf. What was I thinking? This is nuts — playing 18 holes with Paul, the Chief Operating Officer (COO) of one of my major clients? He is an outstanding golfer; I, on the other hand, barely know what end of the club to use. How did I get myself into this situation? Thinking back a few weeks, I thought about how it all started with a call from Frank ...

The vibration jolted me to attention; the cell phone on my side alerted me to a call. It was Frank. Frank was the Chief Executive Officer (CEO) of a $5 billion company. He was having "problems" with one of his top executives. Recently promoted to CEO, Frank had worked with Paul for five years, and he had questioned his capabilities for most of those five years. Now as his boss, Frank could do something about it.

As the new CEO, he wanted to be thoughtful and sure of his actions. Yet, at the same time, he didn't want to perpetuate ineffective leadership in the organization. He knew that the whole team was watching how he would deal with Paul. The corporate grapevine was speculating that Frank's predecessor was terminated for his indecisiveness and weak leadership. Frank knew he was being judged closely. His next move would determine whether or not he gained the team's respect as

CEO and would indeed set the tone for his tenure as the leader. A lot was riding on this one situation for both Frank and Paul.

I had met Frank while facilitating a top-to-top session between his company and a major vendor. At the end of the two-day session, Frank approached me and thanked me for guiding them through some sticky issues. Since that meeting, Frank would call on me to help him with various business issues or projects.

"So, Sam, (Sam was short for Samantha) do you think you can help?" Frank asked. I responded, "I don't know." Having assisted Frank for several years, I think he appreciated my honesty or at least found it refreshing.

The higher up in the organization, in theory, the more you should be surrounded by greater intelligence, experience and truth. I'll not comment on intelligence or experience. However, the truth tends to have an inverse relationship. It is harder and harder for senior executives to get to the truth about what is happening in their organizations. That irony was not lost on Frank. He was diligent about uncovering the facts, getting to the real truth, and asking the tough questions. He never punished people for bringing "bad news." And he was not afraid to subordinate his ego to get to the bottom of things. It unnerved some people. I applauded it.

Fortunately for me, Paul was not an unknown commodity. I had met Paul in the course of my consulting work. Facilitating strategic planning sessions, leading process re-engineering efforts, managing special projects, I found Paul to be both intelligent and highly committed to the company. As COO, Paul was known for running a very "tight ship." Unfortunately, there clearly was a disconnect between him and Frank.

I knew that this assignment would not be easy. Telling the truth and asking the hard questions, requires courage and diplomacy. In order to be effective, all my talents as consultant, advisor and "organizational therapist" would be needed.

"Tell me, what prompted this call?" I asked. Twenty minutes later Frank was still painting the picture. The frustration in his voice was obvious. A genuine people person, he cared about Paul and what it would do to him and to his family if Frank terminated him. At the same time, I had no doubt about Frank's ability to make difficult decisions. He is a very strong, forceful and take-no-prisoners kind of guy; but that doesn't mean he can't empathize and feel badly about such a potentially painful event for Paul.

It brought to mind a situation very early in my career. I was working for an extremely "tough" manager. You know the kind — intimidates and frightens everyone. On a particular occasion, I knew that he had to terminate several people; I asked him how *he* was doing. I don't know exactly why I ventured to ask him, given our boss-underling relationship. He surprisingly confided in me that he had been awake the whole night, vomiting in anticipation of firing these three people. Strangely, he and I became close friends. In truth, he was one of the nicest, kindest people. Of course, I am sure those three people would not have agreed; but it highlighted that a tough exterior sometimes may hide a compassionate interior.

"So, Frank what are you asking me to do? Do you want me to find out if he is salvageable? Or, have you already made the decision to let Paul go? Clearly, you do not need my permission to terminate Paul."

"I don't know." Frank snapped. "Paul just always says the wrong thing. He creates a lot of turnover in his group — turnover that we can't afford! I can't tell you the number of good employees who have come into my office after hours and shared their frustrations about working for Paul. And I do mean 'for' not 'with.' I can almost predict that within two to three months that employee will be gone. Naturally, as CEO these after-hours chats have slowed, but the frustration hasn't diminished among his people. Despite the economy, it is getting harder and harder to find good people. I can't have a top executive driving out our best resources! How can we build for the future if we have no leadership depth in such a critical area?"

"Maybe you should send Paul to the competition — it could be just the advantage you need. He could drive all their good people to you!" I couldn't resist a little levity. Frank needed it. I could hear the relief in his laughter.

"You're right. I bet their recruiter just sits outside our building waiting for Paul's people to resign. What an easy job he has. We screen and train their recruits. Do you think we can request a commission? It could be a whole new revenue stream for us."

Frank turned serious again, "I have tried talking to Paul several times, encouraging him to be more 'people-y.' He seems to be better for a little while, and then — BAM — we are right back to the same old Paul."

Building up a head of steam, Frank continued, "Plus, he never seems to be on-board. In meetings, he always 'hoses' the new ideas. Comes up with all sorts of reasons why it won't work. He just sucks all the oxygen out of the room. I'm sure he'd prefer we not make any changes and just let the market march right by us. I really don't know how he ever got to such a senior level."

"Clearly, you and others find Paul a challenge, to put

it mildly," I acknowledged. I let that settle for a moment, and then redirected, "I noticed you have not questioned his intelligence. I've had a few dealings with Paul and find him extremely sharp. What does he do well? Are there any positives?" I asked.

"Well, he knows his stuff. He is very technical and very thorough. When he does get on-board, he will see things to completion. But then he micro manages too much. Drives all his subordinates nuts. Sorry ... you wanted me to stay on the positives."

"So given the Paul situation, what would be the optimal outcome in your mind?" I pushed.

"Well, the best result would be if Paul became the quintessential leader − inspiring others to greatness." Frank replied.

"Well, let's not lose all means of sanity." I quipped. "Just like you and me, Paul was wired at a very early age. He is what he is. He can't change himself, and we certainly can't change him."

"So, you're telling me there is no hope," Frank asked.

"Not exactly. I said 'not exactly,' because I think we can work together to help Paul make some adjustments. We need to identify and understand does he have what it takes? And does he know what to do with it? In truth, we are asking a lot. He is a seasoned manager that we are now trying to determine if he can make the quantum step to leader. And if not leader, can we make him a more effective manager. These are big questions."

With a heavy sigh, Frank added: "You are right ... this is big. I am hoping for a major transformation from an old-school taskmaster to an inspiring leader. Is that even possible at this point?"

"That's why I said, 'I don't know.' It is a lot to ask. As part of the coaching, we need to enlighten him and his team as to his natural styles and strengths — how he communicates, approaches work, delegates, etc. Also, we should focus not just on Paul; the goal is to make his whole team high performing. So, maybe any leadership holes that Paul has can be filled by others on his team. I don't think I have ever found a leader who had the complete package ... uh, except you of course!"

"Good catch! It is tough being perfect," Frank grinned.

"No comment ..."

Turning serious again, "That's sounds great; but it also sounds unobtainable." Frank said with ambivalence.

"Well, he may never become the perfect leader in your eyes. And we may conclude at some point that Paul is just not the right fit even with some adjustments. You may ultimately need 'to *graduate*' him (I despised the word fire); but, I know Paul a bit, and I think we can make some major strides." Without skipping a beat, I added, "Now, just to underscore, I said, 'I think WE can work together.' That means *you* are critical to this effort. You also will need to be enlightened not only about Paul's natural styles, but also your own. Your style filters the way you see the world — how you interpret and respond to Paul and anyone else for that matter. For me to accept this 'challenge' I need your commitment of time and open-mindedness."

"How much time?"

"To be honest, a fair amount. I will need some time with you, maybe a couple of hours a week to start. But it doesn't have to be in the office. Plus, I will want you to take two quick surveys. And at some point, we will want to take your leadership team off-site for a performance workshop." I let that sink in.

Frank mulled it over, "Well, the cost of interviewing, selecting, and integrating a replacement at his level is astronomical. And the business disruption and productivity loss is no small amount either. I don't even want to think about how big his golden parachute is. Plus, if we hire someone who doesn't fit the position, we are right back to square one. So, clearly I need to invest time in this. We just need to be quick, or as quick as possible. I need to know that we are making progress, and I need for others to see that we are not avoiding the Paul situation." Not missing a beat, Frank continued, "All right, how do we start? What do I need to do?"

"I'll call Jan and get on your schedule ASAP. By the time we meet, I will have an overview of our plan and approach. In the meantime, I will set up access for you to take those two surveys — I promise they are quick. It should take you only five to 10 minutes for each ... really."

"OK, I will take them over the weekend." After a deep exhale, Frank relaxed a bit. "And thanks. I really want to do what is right." I could hear the relief in his voice. Not that we had solved anything as of yet, but that he had a partner in understanding and working on the problem. As many CEOs will confide, it can be a very isolating job.

"Don't thank me yet. The result may still necessitate you 'to *graduate*' Paul."

COACH AND THERAPIST

The following Monday, I was waiting to meet Frank to outline the "Paul Plan." My mind was wandering a bit since Frank was late. I was thinking about one of my earliest management lessons from my dad. Having grown up in a family business, I learned from a very early age the importance of knowing and respecting your employees. My father always promoted and proved that if you treat people with respect and expect them to do the right things, they will act with respect and they will do the right things. On occasion you may get one "bad apple," but it shouldn't change how you work with all the others. Maybe it sounds naïve, but he was right. It was an important lesson for me to learn at a young age.

With my thoughts returning to Paul, I knew we needed to make sure we treated him with respect and to do right by him and the company. With Paul there was a lot of "moving parts." We had Paul himself. Who was he really? What were his natural strengths? What motivated him to behave the way he did? Then we had his team. Who worked with (for) him? What were their strengths and motivations and how were their various interactions? And certainly we can not forget Frank and the rest of Frank's leadership team. There was a lot to think about.

How much of Paul was hard wired (innate) and how much was conditional (learned)? The pragmatic conclusion is that it didn't really matter. *He is what he is.* The things we do have control over are learning who we are, understanding how we naturally respond and why, and working to moderate and adjust our behavior as best we can ... knowing full well, that when under pressure or stress, we revert to our natural behaviors. The burning questions were: Would Paul be open to understanding himself better? Would he be willing to try and moderate some of his natural behaviors? And would Frank have the patience and provide the support necessary?

Jan snapped me out of my concentration, "Frank, just called. He'll be here in five minutes."

"So when I hear the four-wheel skid into the parking lot, I will know he has arrived, right?"

She chuckled, "He can't hide his intensity and zest

for life, now can he?" Jan had worked with Frank for 10 years, moving with him when he came here. She was like the character 'Radar' from MASH. She anticipated his needs, followed through on his assignments, covered his back, and provided a great sounding board. She was invaluable. They were a great team.

No less than five minutes later, Frank blew into the office. The pace and urgency of the whole office began to increase as soon as he got within one mile of the building. Phones started ringing more, email inboxes started pinging more, people started rushing around more — you can't help but wonder, did productivity go up or just the activity level?

"Sam, sorry to make you wait. Running late. Caught on a bloody conference call with Dubai, which put me behind for a meeting with my NY investors, blah, blah, blah. You know how it goes. Jan, anything on fire that I need to know about?"

"Nope ... nothing that either can't wait or burn itself out on its own." Frank bent his head down peered over his volume-discount reading glasses, and shot a glance at Jan. Her eyes confirmed that all was OK. He could take a breath and deal with whatever later.

Turning to me, Frank asked, "How are you doing? Hey, we had a great time with you and Dave at the club

Saturday night. I am now thinking about putting a bocce ball court in at the house. What do you think?"

Following him into his expansive office, I responded, "Dave and I love it. How many games can you play where you *are required* to drink red wine and argue? It's our kind of game."

It was 9:00 a.m. – and he had already put in a half-day's work. Frank collapsed into his overstuffed leather chair and stretched out his legs. I staked out the leather couch as my territory. Being rather short, it was not the most comfortable seat. I think top executives must have their offices furnished through the NBA. If I actually sat straight back, my feet wouldn't just be off the ground, my legs would shoot straight out and the bottom of my shoes would be facing Frank ... not the most professional image.

"Frank, I know you are busy, so I will be as quick and concise as you need me to be. There are two things on my agenda. First, I would like to debrief the results from your behavioral survey and review the job survey you did on Paul's job. Second, I would like to review the Paul Plan with you. Anything on your agenda?"

"You mean you don't have the Paul thing fixed already ... it's been two business days plus a whole weekend since we started this covert operation," Frank jibed.

"Well, if we fixed him that quickly I wouldn't be able to

charge you as much. So, I have slowed down the process."

"Good thinking. As far as the agenda, yes I have a couple of things I want to discuss, but let's start with your topics first. Plus, I am assuming we are not going to spend much time on me. It is Paul who is the focus. At the same time, I know you have a method to your madness. So, I will go along unless I really think we are off course. Please proceed."

For the next 15 minutes, I proceeded to share Frank's survey results. As soon as Frank requested my help with Paul, I knew that I would need some fast and highly accurate tools to get quickly to the root of both Frank and Paul's styles. I fortunately have some secret weapons. With more than 25 years in management and organizational development, I had stumbled onto some talent management analytics that were truly incredible. Much to my amazement, they were not well known in the industry; but those people and businesses who did know about them were absolutely dedicated to using them ... they became part of the fabric for leading and managing. When they would move to a new company, they would implement the analytics so that they could use accurate data to align the organization. Literally, through word-of-mouth, these tools are used by thousands of companies worldwide ... and still they are one of the best-kept secrets in business. Developed and in use for decades, my skepticism was further calmed by the fact that a team from one of the most prestigious medical schools regularly checked their validity and reliability. It was consequently not a concern to apply the tools into such a critical and highly visible situation, as I had many years using them and seeing the value and power they provided in business. Plus, I had been planning on introducing Frank to some of them, and this situation offered the perfect opportunity.

"Frank, I know you pretty well, yet your survey results provided much greater insight into your motivations and behaviors ... and the intensity by which we will see those behaviors. Looking at the graphs, I know they don't mean much to you, but let me describe what they depict." I continued to share Frank's results with him. An extremely persuasive, outgoing, extrovert, he quickly connects with people and 'reads' people well. He is genuinely interested in people and has empathy for them. He uses that knowledge and charisma to get people to do things that he needs or wants done. His next greatest strength is his focus on the big picture and achieving results. He needs to win and combined with his people focus, he strives for the team and company to win. These two top strengths were so intense (amplified by his impatience and urgency), it was clear that at times he could be aggressive and potentially volatile. When I touched on that, Frank responded.

"You know, early in my career, I was pretty volatile. And yes, some might say a bit aggressive or belligerent," Frank admitted. "But I had to push hard to get things done; however, over the years, I have definitely controlled that and have changed."

"Great," I said. Believing that Frank truly does control and moderate that aggressiveness more now; however, I knew that it does still emerge on occasion. I actually saw it not too long ago. We were out to dinner with his entire leadership team after a day-long planning session. I was exhausted after having facilitated the 10-hour session. So I enjoyed quietly listening to the conversation and observing the dynamics. Frank was leading the discussion — and given his profile, he was naturally trying to sell the team on something. I don't recall on what it was he was trying to convince everyone, but as the team pushed back, the louder and more aggressive his points became. Ultimately, the rest of the table got very quiet while Frank dominated the conversation, moving from a selling to a telling style. I am sure Frank wouldn't even remember the incident, but I bet all his managers do. And I bet if I had asked Frank about his behavior then, he would not have identified it as aggressive or belligerent;

but I bet his managers would have. So, working with Frank was going to be as important as working with Paul.

After debriefing Frank about his results from the behavioral survey, I could tell he was blown away. "WOW! How did you get all of that from the survey? I have to say, it was so quick, I really wasn't expecting much. At my previous company, they required all of the senior managers to go through a battery of tests. I spent nearly a week off-site being dissected by a bunch of psychologists. It was fascinating and torturous at the same time; but you nailed me in five minutes what it took them four days and more than $20,000 to do — and you identified things that no one could have possibly known. Incredible. No wonder you called it a *debrief!* Are you sure you didn't interrogate Judy (Frank's wife of 22 years) during bocce ball on Saturday night?"

"Nope ... sorry, you weren't the topic of our discussion. I know it is amazing. The tools are incredibly accurate. And the application in business is only limited by our thinking. So you can see why I am so excited about sharing them with my clients. And the best news is that we can incorporate these analytics into the company so that your leaders and managers improve how to tie and align business goals and talent management. When we are done with the Paul discussion, let's talk about how to introduce them into the company and when we can train your leadership team. However, if it is OK with you, let's focus now on the other survey you took. The one that you completed for the COO position (the job currently held by Paul)."

"Sounds good." Still shaking his head, Frank couldn't contain is astonishment. "WOW, I am still amazed. Hey, can you have Jan take this? Better still have Judy take it too. But yes, let's go on."

"Sure." Moving on, "OK, now that you have a bit of an understanding of how to read the graphs, notice the job graph for Paul's job. It was created as a result of your input. Notice that it is different than your own personal graph? Which tells us that you feel different strengths are needed for the COO position."

"So what behaviors or strengths as you call them does it describe? And what are the differences?" Frank's curiosity continued to peak.

From Frank's results, it was clear that he felt the COO needed to be a people person, someone who could develop and engage a team; while at the same time, someone who could be strategic, as well as analytical and technical. Frank's results also described the need for a good planner; a person who is thorough, accurate, follows through, a calculated risk taker; not a person who would just try it and see; a person who thought about the consequences and protected the company from risk. Bottom-line, someone with some strengths similar to Frank and some very different ones as well.

"You know that is the best job description I have ever read. It clearly articulates how the job should be performed. Not so cut and dry like most traditional descriptions that outline job responsibilities, required experience and education – the past and the what, not the 'how' ... very interesting."

"I agree." I added, "We can easily take this description as the basis for the job and then add responsibilities, required experience and education. So, now you have a full picture of what the job is – what experience and knowledge is needed; what has to be done; and how to perform it effectively. There is a lot more to this – you and your team will be amazed. The major point for us is that we can use these tools in multiple ways – to better understand how you see Paul; how you expect him to perform; how different he is from you and possibly from what you expect, as well as how best to coach him. It lets us accelerate the process and get to some root issues very quickly. Cool, huh?"

"Absolutely! I think you should do my whole team as soon as possible ... but back to Paul. So now what is the next step?" Frank's drive for results was showing.

"Well, let's walk through the plan ... what you need to do, what I need to do, etc. I just want to caution you again, we're not going to change Paul. We are going to help him moderate some of his strengths and highlight others as needed. It will take time. And it may not even work. Plus, we need to work on how you interact with him; how you communicate and set the tone — that will be critical." As much as I said these words, I knew they were falling on deaf ears at this point. Frank was still a believer of the "we-can-change school." And more surprisingly, he may even have enrolled in the "we-believe-we-can-change-others school." In my mind, it is insanity. He probably also subscribed to the annual evaluation as a great method to change someone.

Somewhere along the management evolution, we took an irrational detour. I suspect like many things the intentions were honorable, but the application went haywire — it is best illustrated by the notorious *annual-evaluation* process. (Whenever I say that term, I hear organ music striking in the background from some scary "B" monster movie.) It brings chills to the person being evaluated and brings anxiety to the manager giving it. Companies spend millions and millions of dollars on antiquated processes that I judge provide no or negative ROI. Why do we do it? Why don't we fix it? If it is intended to encourage, energize and focus employees, why does it do the opposite? And yes I know some folks will disagree; but, I bet those who disagree are the few that do get encouragement, are energized, and gain a better focus as a result. They are the lucky few who have leaders. Having burned through a large volume of managers, I can recall only one person in all my years that I would classify as a leader.

If it weren't so personally devastating to many, the evaluation process would be almost comical. Generally, the first part of the game for the evaluator is to try and figure out who to place in the various categories in terms of performance. I came from one of the "Big 8" firms (at least it was eight when I started, now six, four, whatever) where we employed a mathematical matrix — leave it to accountants to remove all humanity from a human process. The game became clear for the evaluators — you "won" the game by having only a few top performers. To make big points in the game, it was always prudent to have some "good" non-performers in your pocket.

Once you had all your numbers figured out, it all had to average to the right total dollar that you were allotted and the right performance ranking percentage. Heaven help you if you had too many "A" performers — that just wouldn't fly. Remember, we are a bell-curve society! Your numbers would be uploaded and combined with everyone else's, reports would be generated, and late-night, smoke-filled meetings would be convened. If white smoke emerged from the meeting, we could proceed. If not, the process would be bounced back and some closed door counseling sessions with your manager to get the numbers right would occur. The process would take weeks — and we did it twice a year.

Of course, the next steps were for the manager to write up his or her report on the employee, to schedule a meeting, and then have "the discussion." It didn't matter that the manager may have had only a few hours of interaction with the employee over the course of the year, you were expected to provide insightful and helpful criticism. R-R-R-i-g-h-t ...

To quote Voltaire, "What is history? It is the lie that everyone agrees upon." With regard to the annual evaluation system, in my estimation, it is the absurd process that we convince each other brings value.

As a consultant, my mission is to help managers stop the insanity and to become more effective leaders and managers. In theory, shouldn't we strive to create a team of all "A" performers? Shouldn't we be rewarded for that? Shouldn't we stop trying to fix someone's weaknesses? (I have tried to fix mine for many, many years with no success; how could someone else possibly expect "to fix" me?)

Again, I do believe we can make adjustments, approach people through their strengths and get some movement in behavior and results; but at the end of the day, those adjustments are consciously made. They take energy and constant thought on the part of the person who is adjusting.

Instead, shouldn't we try to understand someone's strengths and match them to the job that needs those strengths? And quit worrying about weaknesses or trying to fix something that we can't possibly control? I don't know … it just seems a more rational way to go. And there are tools that can help us do that.

So my attempt with Frank and Paul was to stop the insanity. Maybe the real insanity was me trying!

ARE YOU CRAZY?

Having outlined the plan to Frank, he was in full agreement. As promised, he talked with Paul about me coaching him. As expected, Paul was reluctant. A seasoned business man, industry expert, what could an outside consultant possibly offer him? Despite his reservations, he was astute enough to know that he and Frank had issues. So, he chose not to make meeting with me a battle. He took both surveys as requested and made time on his calendar.

No one in the entire company had a cleaner more organized office than Paul. No paper was out of place. No picture, diploma or award hanging on the wall was out of alignment. No file or drawer even slightly left open. His desk was obsessively clean — not even a scratch or smudge from use. I am sure he would have had an allergic reaction to my office ... shuffled papers on the desk, a pile of "to-read" periodicals precariously balanced, numerous wires exposed for all the technology gadgets ... nothing that was totally appalling, but clearly not to Paul's standards.

Fortunately, I had Paul's survey results with me. Of course, I knew him somewhat, but the graphs painted a much clearer picture. You did not want to be late to a meeting with Paul. As my father-in-law (a professional salesman now in his eighties who continues to call on customers) always says, "If you can't be on time, then be early." Late would definitely not cut it with Paul.

Knowing from his survey that he would be very skeptical, I gently and confidently walked him through his results, making sure that I covered the history and research upon which the tools were based. He had many great strengths — strategic, competitive (not unlike Frank). He was analytical and technical, more focused on tasks and things than on people (no surprise); driven for results, fast-paced, thrived on challenge. And overall, he wants (needs) to do things right, requires clear structure, details and facts.

It was also clear from his results that he was hearing the message or feeling the pressure from Frank to be more "people-focused." He was *trying* to be more tolerant. The survey also highlighted that he was feeling rather disconnected or not energized by the work and most likely was questioning his role going forward. Given the situation with Frank, it was only logical.

I could see Paul physically relax a bit. He now knew that I understood his strengths, and he confided that he felt relieved to have someone with whom to share his concerns. I promised that our discussions were confidential; but that at some point, I needed to bring him and Frank together.

I walked him through the plan, but reinforced that we most likely would consciously deviate from it as needed:

Steps	Goal/Purpose
1. Frank to talk to Paul	Introduce idea of Sam coaching Paul.
2. Frank and Paul take talent management survey; Sam debrief	Identify and understand similar and different work styles, strengths, etc.
3. Frank take survey for COO	Understand Frank's job expectations of Paul.
4. Sam interview Paul's direct reports	Confirm/refute situation per their perspective.

Steps	Goal/Purpose
5. Sam to coach/ meet with Paul	Understand Paul's leadership perspective and to provide a framework so that we can analyze what adjustments he should make.
6. Conduct an offsite session with Paul and his team	Develop a greater understanding amongst the team; increase overall performance.
7. Ongoing coaching/ support for Paul	For the first few weeks, provide specific coaching sessions; progress to monthly or as requested.
8. License and train Frank and his direct reports in behavioral leadership approach and application of analytics	Develop a greater understanding amongst the team; increase overall performance; transfer knowledge (provide the pole, not just a fish).
9. Ongoing coaching and support for Frank and his team	Ensure that holistic understanding and support occurs; build internal capability so it is self-sustaining.

Paul agreed with the plan and was pleased that it took a holistic approach to improving work relationships and performance. The interactions and interdependencies of all needed to be included and addressed.

To ensure that Paul wasn't just providing a gratuitous acceptance of the plan, I tested him with a no-holds-barred discussion about why I was here. "Paul, I know that you are intelligent and perceptive. And even your survey results cannot hide that you are concerned about the current situation with Frank. Something has to be done to get you two working effectively together and complementing each other's strengths or Frank will pull the trigger. Regardless of your many years and successes with the company, the Board is firmly behind Frank and will certainly not intervene as he builds his team for the future."

"On the other hand," I continued, "you may have already made a determination to leave. If so, that is clearly your decision. In that case, instead of me coaching you and Frank, use me to broker a deal in terms of timing, etc., between you and him. It is your decision."

I clearly hit a chord. "No, no, no. I don't want to leave. My DNA is in this company. I want to stay, but I am so frustrated. Frank and I are so different. Having to deal with Frank as the new CEO, rumors that my team is criticizing me behind my back, employees going to competitors for more money, it is just getting to be too much. Good lord, it is just about the business, why has everyone turned into such whining babies all of sudden?" Paul moaned.

After another 20 minutes of venting and hearing all of the pent-up issues, we were both drained. My goal was to open up "Pandora's Box" — mission accomplished. I was staring at the raw contents of Paul's inner frustrations.

"Paul, I propose that we stop here for today, but let's plan some time to get together and talk about your leadership style, and how to make your team and your relationship with Frank more positive and effective. What is your schedule like over the next two weeks?"

"Not good. I am in regional review meetings all the rest of this week and Monday I leave for India."

"Hmmm." At that point I noticed a carefully placed golf putter sitting in the corner almost out of sight. Paul was known as an outstanding golfer. Seeing his survey results, it made sense. Anything Paul took on, he would do perfectly; he would study, practice and become an expert. He didn't do anything half-baked. I, on the other hand, was occasionally dragged onto the golf course by my husband. Whereas I played pathetically once or twice a year, Paul played emphatically at least twice a week.

This was one of those times when my mouth started

going and my mind was yelling stop — *don't be nuts! Are you insane? Don't suggest it!* "Paul, you know it would be best if we scheduled something outside of the office. How about 18 holes on Saturday?" Now you have done it; your only hope is that he is busy. Please, if there is a god in heaven, say no.

"That actually will work for me. I am in a tournament on Sunday, so that will help me tune-up on Saturday. I will have Fran call and make reservations. I'll see if we can get an 8:00 a.m. tee time. Sound OK?"

"Yes, great." *What am I saying?* It isn't that I am afraid to lose or play poorly in front of him, rather, do I really want to frustrate and/or embarrass him at his club with my 120 golf score — and that's just on the front 9! What have I done?!

An email from Paul's Executive Assistant, Fran, was waiting for me by the time I got back to my office. *Ugh, lucky me.* The club had an 8:20 a.m. tee time available on Saturday. Paul would meet me their Saturday morning at 7:30 a.m., which would give us time for a quick breakfast and a much-needed warm up.

THE WARM-UP

That is why today I find myself driving to the country club in a panic — hoping that my golf game doesn't embarrass me and that Paul is open to leadership coaching.

Arriving at the club, I cautiously walk into the golf shop. The serious business golfers are out Saturday morning. I was just waiting for someone to tap me on the shoulder and say, "Honey, are you sure you should be here?"

I see Paul outside on the putting green practicing. He sees me and waves me over.

He seems relaxed and more jovial than his office persona. "I am ready for my first lesson; but how about a quick breakfast before we start."

"Sounds good to me. Anything I can do to avoid the inevitable embarrassment is a plus. Should I go and apologize to the club president now or wait till after the damage is done? Where is the course marshal? I need to bribe him before we start."

"Oh, it won't be that bad. You give me pointers on how to improve my leadership, and I'll help you with your golf game. How is that for a deal?" He offered.

Sitting in the club grill, I ask Paul about his background. More of the picture is coming into view. Paul started 24 years ago as a bright college intern with the company. He learned everything from the ground up and was quickly recognized for his depth of knowledge and attention to detail. Valuing his expertise, the company promoted him into management, yet he also was frequently moved from managing teams to researching special projects. When I ask him if he requested those projects, he recalls that he usually was assigned. His boss at the time would provide a compelling story and convince him that his expertise was critical. I ask him if he thought the reason he might have been moved into research projects was to get him away from managing people. He cocks his head, begins to say something then stops, and lets out a breath. A few long moments later, he says, "Hmmm. I don't know. I never thought about that. Maybe ... "

To drive home the point, "As you know, I interviewed some of your team to gain their perspective. Obviously, if I am going to help, I need to know what your team and others think. Bottom-line, everyone respects your knowledge and expertise. However, your leadership style is not at the same caliber. And I am not saying that you need to become Mr. Sweetness and sing 'Kum-ba-ya ' at the end of each staff meeting; but I think there are some things that we can do to leverage and moderate your style in order to be a more effective leader ... can you handle some candid coaching?"

"It just feels strange that after 24 years and a pretty impressive career, I am getting coached on how to manage people. I have managed hundreds of employees and have gotten good results."

"No one is discounting that. However, the goal here is to improve your leadership style so that you can achieve even greater results. And not unlike golf, I suspect you are always learning, always practicing, always working to improve your stroke and your game. Even the top golfers in the world practice. Again, it is totally your choice whether or not to proceed."

"OK. You already dissected me the other day. We may as well go all the way. Just know that I may mutiny at any point."

"From your survey results, I already predicted that." After sharing a quick laugh, I continued. "Here is my thought. As we play golf, I thought I would use it as a metaphor for leadership. So hopefully, you don't mind a bit of fun. Remember the deal — you can instruct me on golf and I can instruct you on leadership. And to be honest, I hold out more hope for you than me."

"Sounds good. Just don't screw up *my* handicap!"

Milling around the 1st tee were a few other foursomes. We moved off to the side, so as not to disturb the others. I began the first lesson. Being a true golf novice it wasn't difficult to start. "What does it take to play golf? What do you need in order to play?" I asked.

Paul looked at me strangely, thought a moment then confirmed, "This is your instruction method, right? OK. Well, you need a golf course or a place to play, golf clubs and a ball; as you get more sophisticated, a well-maintained course, golf bag with all your clubs, golf shoes, glove and clear rules. Oh, let me add, desire and time."

"So, basically, there are some key elements you need. You can't just decide to go and play. Even at the most elementary level, you would have to get a stick and a ball and decide that you are targeting a hole."

"Exactly," Paul replied, rolling his eyes. He couldn't hide the fact that he was already dreading these 18 holes and thinking that it was going to be the longest golf day of his life.

"Basically, you have consciously assembled the fundamentals so that you can play golf. Which is the same in leadership ... except that many leaders don't consciously think about or address the fundamentals or at least to the degree they should."

"I'm not sure I am following," Paul quizzed.

"I apologize for sounding too 'consultant-y.' It is a professional hazard. Let me show you in the sand trap over here."

Stepping to the practice sand trap, I took out my putter and started to draw in the sand a square box.

"Well I knew it was coming — I don't think I have ever talked to a consultant without them drawing a four-square box." Paul half joked.

"It is true ... we are not allowed to talk to clients without at least several of these at the ready."

"Ok, let's hear it ... wait you are breaking rules. You have six boxes. Are you sure that is allowed? Are you risking being tossed out of the consultant's club?"

I couldn't blame Paul; he was right. He had probably sat through countless presentations, meetings and conferences that either started or ended with the topic being reduced to a four-square box. I hated to be lumped into that group, but I promised him that I would go much deeper through the course of the day.

Unshaken, I continued, "I break leadership into two buckets or questions: 1. Do you have what it takes? And 2. Do you know what to do with it? Many people have parts of one and/or the other, but truly great leaders have most or all of both. They are unique. As we go through our sessions together, this framework might be helpful. I apologize that it is expanded to six boxes ... however that justifies my rates." I teased, though I think Paul took it seriously.

"If you think about leadership, some people may have all the fundamentals, the capability. Yet, they are not effective, don't get results. And on the flipside, some people can be very effective, but cannot sustain it. They are missing the foundation or fundamentals as I call it. It explains a lot

CAPABILITY — Do you have what it takes?	High Potential	Leader
	Moderate Potential	Manager
	Low Potential	Worker

EFFECTIVENESS ⟶
Do you know what to do with it?

when you think about bosses you encountered in the past or read about CEOs who publicly flame out."

Paul thought for a moment. "Where do you think I am?"

"I have no idea ... but we will figure it out together. It won't happen all today, but we can start. Still game?" I offered another opt-out point.

"Do I have a choice?"

"Yep, you do; but what is the worst that can happen? You may gain a new perspective, improve your leadership, and spend some time with me. Sounds like a win, win, win! But make no mistake, it may not always be fun."

"Put me in coach, I am ready to play!" With that the starter called us "on deck" for the 1st tee.

THE FRONT NINE: DO YOU HAVE WHAT IT TAKES?

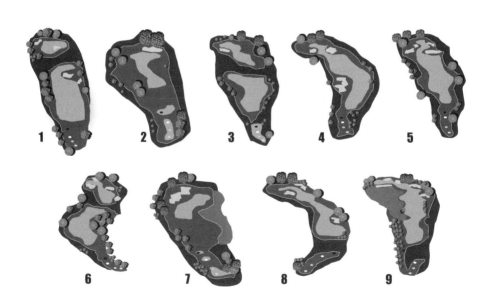

CAPABILITY AND EFFECTIVENESS: THE DREADED 1ST TEE

After pulling out his driver, Paul walked over to shake hands with the two members of our club-arranged foursome. As with most every golf course in the country, it was virtually impossible to have just two golfers play a round of golf by themselves on a Saturday morning. Paul politely introduced me to the two men. Jim was the EVP of Sales for a successful software company and had brought as his guest Mario, the CIO of a growing regional bank. Again, my golf anxiety took a major jump while listening to their golf banter. As expected, Jim and Mario typically played more golf in a week than I did in a year. It was definitely going to be a long day for all of us.

After a little chatter about the course, the weather, and a few self-effacing remarks about one's current game, it was our turn at the 1st tee. If golf really wanted to encourage more players, they would put the 1st tee in a remote location and would prevent others from watching ... I realize that makes no sense; but the 1st tee is scary. Face it ... you don't have your golf rhythm going yet (if ever), probably muscles are still too tight, and the palms are sweating, which screws up your grip.

I will never forget my most memorable 1st tee or should I say my husband's. For some ungodly reason, several years ago, we got an early morning tee time on New Year's Day with two close friends. Sam and the three amigos planned to start the year off right (clearly they out voted me on what was the best way to start off the new year).

We were running late, but thankfully the course was on a frost hold. Finally, we were called to the tee. Dave bravely offered to go first. He took forever to approach the ball, study the fairway, etc., etc. With a good smack of the ball, it flew forward, hit a sign not more than 20 feet in front of him, and bounced back behind the 1st tee, nearly taking out a good portion of the gallery. Naturally, we tried to hold it together with not much success. The uninjured gallery doubled over attempting to hide their laughter as well. Any possible decorum was gone.

Not to be outdone, Tim, the next amigo in the four-some, got up, smacked the ball, and did the exact same thing. Talk about shock and awe ... the gallery was roaring. (We hoped they would still appreciate the humor after following us around the rest of the day.) With that Bob and I just hit or threw our balls down the fairway ... best to get out of there before they usher us off the course. Still crying from laughter, we crept off the 1st tee. It was then I realized that golf humor originated from "potty-mouth" adolescent boys! Naturally, we still enjoy reminding Dave of his best 1st tee.

I am hoping with all my might, that I don't replicate Dave's 1st tee here today. Mario stepped up to the tee, addressed the ball, and launched the ball with great precision. Flying 200 yards down the center of the fairway, Mario was clearly pleased with his performance. Next up, Jim took his driver and challenged the men's 356-yard hole. After several retreats, Jim addressed the ball, exhaled, and gave it a powerful whack; delighted that he too had sailed his ball down the fairway where it landed just slightly left and several yards short of Mario's.

Paul, up next, wasted no time. Placing the ball firmly on the tee, checking his angle, he quickly stepped to the ball, took one measured practice swing with his massive driver, and blasted the ball 230 yards just beyond the intruding sand trap. It was a picture-perfect swing, and a picture-perfect placement. "Not bad, considering I still feel a little tight."

OMG ... this is going to be a train wreck. The only question that remains is what will blow first — my frustration or their patience. Oh well, time to just suck it up. With false confidence, I grabbed my driver, walked the plank to the women's tee (310 yards), and hoped for the best. No reason to dwell, just get it over with ... I lined up — angles are everything — addressed the ball, checked my grip, pulled back and swung. For once the "Golf Gods" were smiling on me. Yes, dear, I kept my head down ... the ball flew 160 yards mostly straight. I couldn't have asked for a better shot off the 1st tee. Maybe this wasn't going to be such a "sucky" day after all.

Rushing to the golf cart with more spring in my step than moments earlier and hoping for a "that-a-girl," Paul instead reflected on my two buckets. "You know it makes sense. Even thinking about world-class athletes like Lance Armstrong and Michael Phelps, their bodies are built for their sports — they have what it takes for the sport; but I suspect there are others in this world who have even better-built bodies for the sport, but they are not competing. So when you have the foundation or fundamentals and you know what to do with them, amazing things happen. I realize we are not talking about my lung capacity for leadership, but I think you get what I am saying. In mathematical terms, if you have 100 percent of what it takes and do what you need to do at 100 percent, your results will be stunning. And if you are only 90 percent, maybe you can compensate with the other bucket by pushing to 110 percent; but if you are clearly deficient in one bucket, it would be near impossible to subsidize the other. For example, you couldn't be 50 percent in one and expect the other bucket to make up 150 percent."

"By George, you got it! OK, we are done, let's head to the clubhouse — and I can avoid any golf embarrassments that lie ahead." I mocked relief.

"Hey that was a great stroke. I meant to compliment you. And since we are already here, we may as well play the round. Plus, you promised to go deeper on what is in those two leadership buckets."

Being the furthest away from the hole, the carts made a beeline to my ball, swarming around it as though it were the queen bee. Words of encouragement were offered by Mario and Jim. With 150 yards left to the hole, I chose my 3 wood. With any luck, I might be able to make the green. With a big exhale, head down, and chant playing in my head, I whacked the ball through the grass, veering slightly right and squarely into the sand trap that Paul had so effortlessly avoided.

"OK Coach, suggestions?" I asked as we repositioned the golf carts and waited for Jim and Mario to take their next strokes.

"Actually, your form is good. Try slowing down your stroke a bit."

Jim, left with about 158 yards to the hole, took out his 5 iron and powered the ball to the back of the green, leaving him a long 30-foot putt. Mario also selected his 5 iron and landed his ball just on the right skirt of the green. With an uphill, angular putt, he was facing a real challenge.

Fortunately it was not a links course. This course has a kinder, gentler bunker ... fairly flat, no rope ladder required for egress. Without too much damage, I was able to escape the bunker thanks to some guidance from Paul. "Think of scooping the ball out ... hit behind it ... don't try and kill it ... don't worry, I will watch where it goes." A lucky stroke gently bounced my ball onto the green, leaving me a 10-foot putt. "I'll take it!" My pressure suspended for a few moments, we then waited for Paul's second shot. Selecting his 9 iron for the remaining 126 yards, he checked his angle, looked one last time at the flag, and instructed the ball to find the hole. Like a bird dog it complied and landed 12 feet short, froze and pointed to the target.

"What is your handicap again?" I asked.

"It ranges ... right now it is around eight." He tried to hide his pride.

"Bologna. What is the lowest you've been?"

"I got down to three a few years ago; but with all my travel, I don't get to play as much as I used to."

"Again, bologna." I said while walking with our putters to the green. "You like to win, so I suspect your registered handicap is eight but your game is three or less. You're sandbagging!"

Smiling, Paul said, "Not true." And with that he bowed, "After you."

Running a little fast, my ball seemed to want to stay on the green longer than I had hoped. One strong putt sent my ball jogging past the hole another 10 feet. Oops, I forgot it is better to leave it short. Well, two more putts and I was in ... thankfully. I was feeling pretty good, just three over par; oh yeah, this was just the 1st hole. Jim three putted, which left him one over par, same as Mario. Paul hit a clean stroke to make par and enjoyed an early lead. But I didn't care; the dreaded 1st hole was done.

NANCY L. CLARK

HOW MANY STROKES WAS THAT?

Driving the short distance to the 2nd tee, Paul and I continued our conversation. I proposed to use

> guiding values

the front nine to examine the leadership capabilities and fundamentals or as I called it the "Do-you-have-what-it-takes bucket;" and, leave the back nine to examine leadership capabilities or the "Do-you-know-what-to-do-with-it bucket."

I was pleased that Paul was both relaxed and engaged. Maybe a round of golf wasn't such a bad idea after all. Even my game seemed to be holding its own.

Paul, Mario and Jim all had consistently strong tee shots. On a par 3, 182-yard hole, Paul chose his 4 iron. Impressively, he landed on the green leaving an "easy" four-foot putt. Mario selected his 3 iron and ran the ball straight onto the green, just pin high. With his 3 iron, Jim hit the back of the green narrowly missing the large bunker that invited over strikers. Walking to the ladies tee, my 142 yards seemed doable. I decided to use my 3 wood. On a good day, I might be able to reach the green. I was afraid that if I used my driver and actually connected, I could end up in the bunker near Jim. I was hoping to avoid as many sand traps and water hazards as possible.

Much to my surprise, my ball landed on the green just several feet from Mario's. Unbelievable. Finishing with two putts, my confidence was building.

"Who is the sandbagger now? With all your talk, I thought you would be a nightmare," Paul chided. Mario and Jim joined in the fun, "Yeah ... what's up with that approach stroke?"

"Guys, truly ... I only play a few pathetic times a year. Trust me this won't last ... so don't get hopeful."

Loping back to the cart, I joined Paul. "OK, back to school. What do you believe are the fundamentals for great leadership?"

"Honesty needs to be number one." Paul adamantly offered.

"I agree. And isn't it amazing that so many 'leaders' fall from grace." What happened to their values? Did they ever have them? The list is long and the wake caused by their deeds is beyond tragic. We talked about some of the more notorious ones, Madoff, Ebbers, Skilling among others.

Sample of Misguided Leaders

- Bernard Madoff, founder and former Chairman of Bernard L. Madoff Investment Securities LLC and former Chairman of NASDAQ: Sentenced in July 2009 to the maximum 150 years in federal prison and $170 billion in restitution for what the judge called an "extraordinarily evil" that shook the nations faith in its financial and legal systems. Madoff pled guilty to multiple securities fraud, investment advisor fraud, mail fraud, wire fraud, money laundering, false statements, perjury, making false filings with the SEC, and theft from an employee benefit plan. The self-confessed author of the biggest financial swindle in history is not eligible for parole. However, he can get up to 15 percent off from his original sentence for good behavior, which would still leave him facing at least 127 years.

- Bernard Ebbers, former CEO of WorldCom: Sentenced in July 2005 to 25 years in federal prison. Ebbers was found to be the mastermind behind an $11 billion accounting fraud which ultimately pushed WorldCom into the largest bankruptcy at the time in U.S. history.

The court ordered him to forfeit his Mississippi mansion and an additional $45 million in assets.

- Jeffrey Skilling, former CEO of Enron: Sentenced to 24 years and four months in federal prison and fined in excess $45 million. On February 12, 2001, Jeffrey Skilling was named CEO of Enron, receiving $132 million in a single year from the nation's largest energy giant. Just five years later, Skilling was convicted for securities violations and corporate fraud violations leading to the largest bankruptcy in U.S. history and the loss of 20,000 jobs.

- Dennis Kozlowski, former CEO of Tyco: Sentenced to a maximum of 25 years in state prison for his role in looting hundreds of millions of dollars from Tyco. He was ordered to pay back to Tyco $134 million in stolen money and was fined an additional $70 million.

- John Rigas, former CEO and founder of Adelphia Communications: Sentenced to 15 years in prison in 2005 for his part in the multi-billion dollar fraud scheme that bankrupted the nation's fifth-largest cable company. Riggas' son Timothy, Adelphia's former CFO, was also convicted in the looting of Adelphia and was sentenced to 20 years. Both were convicted on 18 felony counts of conspiracy and fraud.

- Sam Waksal, former CEO and founder of ImClone. Sentenced to seven years and three months for his role in an insider-trading scandal that involved his close friend Martha Stewart. Waksal pleaded guilty to sharing with relatives in 2001, that ImClone's bid to win regulatory approval for its cancer drug, Erbitux, was not going to succeed. This information was not yet known to the public. Waksal also agreed to pay a $4.3 million fine. The drug Erbitux has since been approved by the FDA.

- Joe Nacchio, former CEO of Qwest Communications: Sentenced to six years in prison for making $52 million in illegal stock sales while a multi-billion dollar accounting scandal within Qwest brought the telecommunications giant to near bankruptcy.

- Charles H Keating Jr., former owner of Lincoln Savings and Loan, spent time in jail and ultimately pled guilty to four counts of fraud and admitted taking $1 million from American Continental Corp, parent company of Lincoln, whose failure in 1989 cost taxpayers $3.4 billion. In 1999, a decade later, the court ruled Keating would pay no further fines and would not be returned to prison in exchange for pleading guilty. The government also agreed to dismiss fraud charges against Keating's son, Charles III, as part of plea agreement.

- B. Ramalinga Raju, founder, Satyam Computer Services, Ltd.: Awaiting sentencing and is accused of India's biggest corporate fraud including conspiracy, cheating and forgery. Raju said in January 2009, he overstated the Hyderabad-based software provider's assets by $1 billion and falsified accounts that went undetected for years. He faces a maximum penalty of life in prison if convicted.

Both of us wallowed in thought — did these leaders have no principles? Did they have them only to lose them? Did greed, pressure, ego, all of the above cause their meltdowns? Did they think they would get away with it? Did they think they could "fix" it before it imploded? Madoff admitted he knew he would get caught ... how does one live with that?

We were so engaged in thought and conversation that we hardly noticed playing the 3rd hole. Sometimes distracting my mind away from the game is better. I don't over think the stroke, distance, obstacles, etc. I just hit the ball naturally or as I have been taught. The results are sometimes pleasant surprises.

"You are right Sam; clear strong guiding values are critical in a leader. Real values ... not just convenient values. Values mean nothing if you throw them overboard whenever you hit choppy waters."

"Exactly, you have to hold them true. A leader has to be willing to take the heat now and deal with the consequences. Rather than 'fudging' on the financials or talking in the 'gray' areas, value-based leaders must hold firm. It is the hardest thing and a real test of a true leader."

"OK, I am going to show my age here; but, Frank, remember in the '80's when there was a major scare with Tylenol? Someone tampered with the product which resulted in seven deaths in the Chicago area." At the time, the Chairman of Johnson & Johnson (J&J), James Burke, did not try to hide the problem or ignore it. He immediately formed a task force with only two goals; first, protect people and, two, if possible, save the brand.

From my view he had guiding principles, and he stayed true to them. J&J distributed warnings to hospitals and distributors, halted Tylenol production and advertising, issued a nationwide recall of Tylenol products, and advertised not to consume any products that contained Tylenol. And this all happened within just a few days.

"I remember well. Despite the huge impact, Burke and J&J were praised for their quick action and commitment to the public's safety."

"The good news is that values and strong principles are rewarded. J&J's Tylenol market share collapsed from

35 percent to eight percent, but it rebounded in less than a year. The frightening thing is that there seems to be more examples of leaders sacrificing their values versus examples like James Burke at J&J."

"Sam, let's hope it's because the bad leaders sell more newspapers so we don't hear about all the good leadership deeds."

"I hope you are right."

"So here's a 'small,' but real-life example. I wasn't really looking, but I saw Jim's scorecard. What if I were to tell you, that he marked down a birdie for the 1st hole and par for the 2nd?"

"No ... did he really? I can't believe that. He should be one over, not one under. True? If you are right, I would be very surprised and shocked."

"Would you want to play with him again?" I questioned.

"No." Paul quickly and emphatically responded.

"But it is just a game ... and his score has no impact on you."

"That may be true, but it just makes the game and any conversation tainted. No, if it's true, I would avoid playing with him at all costs. And I certainly would not consider doing business with him. I wouldn't even want to mix with him at any club social events. It just colors my whole view of him."

"Well, the good news is that I did see his scorecard, and he didn't cheat; but consider your reaction. Something as small as a casual golf score can drive good people away. Honesty and integrity are fundamental to leadership. And to make it broader, strong guiding values are fundamental ... great leaders know their values and live their values. Employees, vendors, colleagues can sense those values and can come to depend upon them. It builds a strong foundation of trust."

"Sam, do you think people question my values? Is that a hole in my leadership?"

"No, I don't. I think many managers never become great leaders because they have as you call them 'holes' in their values. I think people know and trust your guiding values. You are very honest and are very transparent ... you say what you mean, and you mean what you say. I think your challenges or 'holes' lay elsewhere, which we will get to soon."

"Oh joy ... I can't wait."

I added, "Of course, I am still questioning your handicap ... that may change my view on your integrity."

As we finished the 3rd hole, I couldn't help but laugh. Paul made par and the rest of us enjoyed one over, including me. But Paul couldn't help himself. Casually sauntering over to Jim and Mario's cart, he was trying to check out Jim's score card clipped to the steering wheel. Thankfully, Jim and Mario didn't catch what he was doing.

"So?" I grilled.

"What?"

"You know what. You wanted to make sure ... you needed proof that he was honest."

"Don't be silly. I just wanted to ask him something."

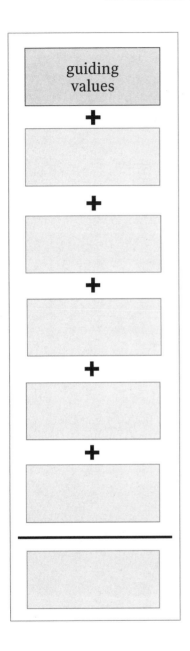

DUFFER OR DRIVER?

The 4th tee was already backed up. "Too many duffers playing today," Jim complained under his breath.

self awareness

"Hey, wait a minute; I strive to reach duffer status," I defended. Thankful that someone else was delaying play, not me.

With one foursome half way down the 345-yard, dog-leg-left fairway, and another foursome preparing to tee off, we had a few minutes to continue the "coaching."

"So, how would you characterize your strengths?" I asked. This had to be trying for Paul. A private, introverted person, he was being a good sport with my questioning and coaching ... at least so far.

After a bit of a pause, "Well, Sam, I have years of experience in the industry and have worked my way up through the company … I know every job there is and what it requires. I know supply chain and operations well."

I interrupted, "Those are life experiences which are different than your strengths. What I am trying to focus upon are your natural behavioral strengths — how you perform or approach the work."

Paul thought deeply, "OK, I am very thorough, like you uncovered in my survey. I hate making mistakes and I hate sloppy work. I have to know the goal and direction, and I don't let obstacles get in my way."

"What else?" Sam prodded.

"I think through issues and challenges. I don't believe in just trying something for the sake of trying something new. I need to analyze and plan things. I like change, but it needs to follow the plan and timelines we set out."

"What about people? And delegation?" I could tell Paul was struggling a bit. It may be surprising that most people do not even know their natural strengths. More times than not, when you ask them, they look at you with a blank stare, or they respond in terms of subject knowledge … which is the wrong answer, as Peter Drucker said. However, if you think about it, it is not that surprising that people don't know their natural strengths. From parents, teachers, spouses and bosses, many of us hear more about what we are not good at as opposed to what we are good at doing. Many go through long careers never knowing or even thinking about who they truly are; what they enjoy or are good at; and what jobs best fit them or what jobs they should avoid.

Stepping upon my soapbox again, think about the annual evaluation process … how much confusion that may cause. "You were good in this area, but you need to improve here." You may believe in your heart that you are delivering a very positive evaluation. But depending upon who is receiving these kind criticisms, you may have just brutally punished him or her. Even if you spent 59 minutes showering the good praise, and only one minute on the improvement suggestion, many people (like Paul) only hear the one minute of non-praise. The other 59 minutes are wiped out.

Unfortunately, the majority of employees go through their careers focusing on their weaknesses, clueless about their strengths. And the dirty, little secret is that we can't change or rewire ourselves. We are who we are; but, and this is a big "but," we can be self aware, understand who we are and how we see the world, work to adjust our styles and behaviors, and achieve better results. It is a conscious effort and adjustment … it is not a rewiring of our natural self. And again, that is what I was starting with Paul.

"Well, I like people," Paul continued. "But I don't suffer fools. People have to perform. If they prove to me they can get results, I will give them more. If they don't get it, they're gone."

"Would you say it takes you time to trust people?" I asked.

"Yes."

"And I would say your focus is more on tasks than politics. It is more what you do versus whom you know." I added.

"Absolutely, it is about results. I can't stand ass-kissers. Excuse my French. But they waste more time socializing, trying to get invited to meetings that they have no business being at, or they take up the hobby of the boss just so that they can rub elbows. If they just put half that effort into doing their jobs, we would be much better off."

Sounds as though I struck a chord. "Yet, Paul, I know you recognize the importance of relationships in business. It isn't all a waste of time?"

"Of course. I know you have to grease the skids, but some people are way off base."

"Agreed. But let's get back to your strengths. I would say you are also very creative. You think and are in your head a lot. And you are not a shallow talker. You like to talk and discuss meaningful things. You generally only will weigh in on things about which you have knowledge or expertise. Plus, I would say you tend to think and then talk while others may talk to think."

Nodding his head, "You are pretty spot on. That's me."

"So, as we approach this 4th tee, what are you thinking about?"

Paul looked at the fairway and then looked at his golf card. "I first think about how many yards to the green? Have they changed the hole placement? Are there new hazards I need to avoid? What are the conditions, wind direction, etc.? Where do I want my first stroke to land? What club would be best? What are others using effectively? My tee placement. So, it is about 345 yards to the green with a dogleg left, where should I lay up ... can I clear the trees and bunkers or should I play it safe? How will the wind impact the flight of the ball?"

"Wow ... you have a lot more processing going on than I do! Right now, watching the other foursome tee off, I am just hoping that we can tee off before another group arrives and is forced to wait and watch us. Ugh ... I am simply hoping that I don't screw up and embarrass myself."

"For a moment, just think though how differently we are approaching the game. Yes, a lot of it has to do with experience and confidence. But let's dissect your approach in light of your strengths. You immediately go to the task at hand — what you need to analyze and know in order to succeed — the distance, hole location, conditions, and so on. Now, you have played this course hundreds of times. And you probably know every member in the club. Let me ask, do you know any of the people teeing off right now?" Paul nodded in the affirmative. "Yet, nowhere in your description did you mention a person, nor have you gone over to talk or acknowledge anyone. Now maybe you did before I arrived today. And I am making no judgments — it is not good or bad, it just is the way you work and think. Now to be fair, you did mention you were observing others to learn what club might be best, but again, I submit it is more about you achieving the goal rather than socializing or connecting to people."

"I know you are not trying to make it sound bad, but when you describe it, I sound a little cold or aloof."

"Again, Paul, this is about self awareness. There is no good or bad, there just 'is.' Everything we do is rooted in our motivations ... you want to get the best score. And although you probably know this golf course as well as the club pro, you do not just grab your trusty driver and swing; you analyze the course each time you play. Those are incredible strengths that can be unbelievably powerful in business."

"So then why do I need a personal coach to help my management style?" Paul's frustration reared its head.

The time was not right to address the difference between management and leadership; we could save that for another day. "That is a fair-enough question. So let's go back — point out the people to me around the tee and in the fairway whom you know and whether or not you talked or acknowledged them this morning."

In a low whisper, Paul pointed out that he knew three of the four people on the tee. He ran into one in the parking lot when he arrived earlier this morning and the other two he nodded or smiled to while waiting at the 1st tee. I asked him what he noticed about the foursome on the tee. After analyzing their golf clubs, practice swings, clothing, hair challenges, he was at a loss. I pointed out that they were all socializing, mixing, quietly talking and teasing each other. Paul admitted he has known most of them for many years and would have joined in the socializing a bit had I not been there. But, in his words, "I am quieter and more serious than most members."

"And there is nothing wrong with that," I reinforced. "However, let's play devil's advocate. How do you think those folks perceived you this morning?"

"They probably think of me as more serious and reserved."

"True. How about the unfair things they may perceive?"

"What do you mean?" Paul quizzed.

"They don't know your full strengths; they only see a bit of you. So, I suspect that they may unfairly perceive you as unfriendly which can then draw thoughts of snobbish, unapproachable, etc. As you are looking at the world through your 'lens' or strengths, others are looking at the world, but through their 'lens' — which may be very, very different from yours. It is not right or wrong, again it just is. I submit, however, to be an effective manager, you need to understand your natural motivations, strengths and behaviors and how they color your perspective. Once someone gains a deep self awareness, he can then better understand others and work to adjust his style to be more effective. Does that make sense?"

"Yes. So in this case what would I do?"

"Well that depends. If you are satisfied with the current relationship or perception of others, you wouldn't adjust or do anything differently. However, if you wanted to build a stronger social relationship with any of those people, you would *consciously* make an effort to be more outgoing. Ask them how they are doing? Connect with them. Whatever. Now, since that is not your natural style, you probably should not go 'over the top,' don't try to be the 'life of the party.' They will sense if it is contrived.

But you could start being a bit more engaging and build from there. It may never be natural, but you can adjust and make a conscious decision to be more outgoing."

"Do you really believe they think I am unfriendly and snobbish?" Paul pondered out loud.

"Good chance." After all the executives I have coached, most of the "Paul's" were shocked to discover that they were perceived so "unfairly."

"So let's connect it to your work life. When you first began in operations, some 24 years ago, you may not have needed to connect and engage with people as much as you do now. What served you well then may be different than what is needed currently. You now have hundreds of people working in your organization. Many of them need or want to feel a connection to you, their leader ... a connection beyond just the work. Not all, but many want a sense that they know you as a person and that you care and take an interest in them and their professional well-being. *Remember, people leave managers first, companies second.* So how do you think they perceive or connect to you?"

"To be honest, they probably perceive me not unlike the foursome ahead of us. I would guess they respect my knowledge, but feel that I am rather distant. And I get where you are going ... some of my direct reports I trust deeply and have worked with for years, but many of my people would or I should say have left me in a hot minute."

"The point here is that you don't have to be a warm, cuddly leader, but you can make some adjustments to reach out and engage more, to strive to be more empathetic — that can go a long way in creating a more positive, productive team and decrease some of your costly turnover. And although your motivation may come more from a need to win (to be a better leader) as opposed to a need for social connection, that's OK. The employees and you both win. Does that make sense?"

"So basically, the bad news is that I cannot really change or rewire who I am; the good news is that if I am aware of my strengths or who I am, I can make conscious decisions or adjustments."

"I might say it a bit differently ... the good news is that you have incredible strengths; the great news is that if you are self aware, you can make conscious decisions to adjust your behavior to achieve desired results. The only bad news is for those who are not self aware or who cannot make conscious decisions to adjust."

"Are you talking about emotional intelligence?"

"Basically, yes. I believe there needs to be more research in this area, but the growing evidence seems to support a direct correlation between emotional intelligence and leadership success."

"It does make sense. If you don't have an awareness of yourself, you will definitely be lower on the emotional scale. You wouldn't know what or how to make the appropriate adjustments to your behavior."

"It brings in situational leadership as well. If you are self aware, understand and recognize other people's strengths, you can evaluate the situation and consciously adjust your behavior to achieve the best outcome."

"For once, all these theories are starting to make sense and how they relate. But, I do see that the foundation to all of that is self awareness and guiding values. I now understand why you gave me that behavioral survey. It quickly and clearly identified and helped me articulate my strengths. In the next few weeks, I would like you to have all my direct reports take it. That may be the best 'gift' I give them."

"I would be happy to do so ... I will debrief each one individually and then you can host a team dynamics session where we examine the whole team together. As you may recall, it is part of our plan, and Frank has committed to training the extended leadership team."

"Great." After a thoughtful pause, Paul continued, "Sam, I really do appreciate you working with me. I am starting to feel better about this whole coaching thing. Maybe it's not such a pain-in-the-ass after all."

"Thanks, I think," willing to accept a compliment however it was delivered.

It was finally time for us to tee off. And no surprise the following foursome had arrived to witness our efforts off the 4th tee. Clearly, I was the only one of our foursome who cared.

Paul, Jim and Mario all hit beautiful shots; all three were grouped nicely about 100-125 yards from the hole. I, on the other hand, decided to make the hole a bit more exciting by heading into the forest. After an embarrassing five-minute search, I chose to sacrifice my bright pink golf ball and join the others with a new ball. I just hope I have enough golf balls with me to make it through 18 holes ... ugh ... we haven't even hit the water hazards yet!

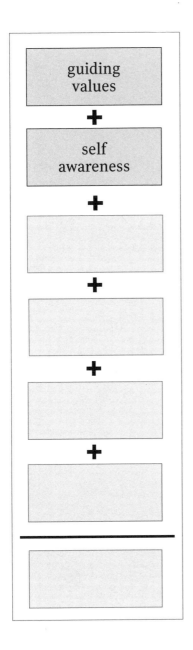

—

IT IS MORE THAN JUST SHOWING UP

"Well, that was ugly. I would like to thank all three of you for your patience on the last hole. I

> listens, learns, engages others

think you can all now agree I wasn't exaggerating my limited playing skills."

"Sam, it wasn't that bad," Paul tried to console. He actually had been quite helpful. After helping me search unsuccessfully for my ball, he had provided some excellent pointers that got me out of two more bad shots. I was happy to survive with a triple bogey; and again Paul led the foursome by making par. He was truly an amazing golfer.

As we prepared for the 5th tee (my slow play on three had allowed the backup to clear ahead of us ... unfortunately a different story for the foursomes behind us), Paul seemed eager to continue our conversation on leadership. "So, Sam, I am starting to understand your fundamental ingredients for leadership. Thus far, we have authentic or guiding values and self awareness or emotional intelligence. What's next?"

"Let's use another golf example. I propose to you that the greatest golfers are great listeners and learners. They are always seeking ways to improve and are testing new approaches to win. The caddy is a perfect example of that. The only time I watch golf on television is when Tiger is playing (however, that may change after his personal indiscretions became public). I love watching him analyze and study the situation, talk and discuss with his caddy, Steve Williams. He is so present, so in the moment — thinking and listening deeply. He and Steve agree on a course of action and then Tiger executes it more effectively than any other player. Make no mistake, Tiger makes the final decision, but he gathers as much data and information that he can. His focus is amazing. He talks and listens to his caddie. And I have heard he has an entourage of coaches, advisors, etc. He is definitely present and in the moment when he is golfing. However, I may be pushing the golf metaphor too far. I actually think comparing sports and business can be unwise."

Paul agreed, "I think all the winning Pro Golfers do

that, some better than others in learning and executing."

"However, in business, I find that many managers don't. Many don't listen and many don't try and learn new things. One in particular comes to mind ... he was the vice president of a 700-person IT department. He literally told me that he didn't believe in taking classes and workshops to learn new approaches or methods and didn't feel the need to read books or articles on leadership. In addition, his whole management style (and I mean management not leadership) was 'if someone needs to talk with me, they can call me.' So not only was he shutting down multiple avenues to learn and improve, but also he wasn't engaging his people to provide a forum for them to come together to learn, exchange ideas, debate possibilities, etc. Talking with his direct reports, they were confused and frustrated; there was no sharing or enhancing of organizational knowledge. His fundamental 'hole' was causing a major organizational leak."

I could tell Paul was thinking as he practiced his swing. Refocused on the game, he stepped up to the 5th tee box; concentrated on the ball and made a giant swing ... the ball rocketed nearly 280 yards. The three of us watched in complete admiration.

Mario stepped up to the tee, "Paul, I hate to have to follow that swing!" Fortunately, Mario did himself justice, a strong swing, just slightly hooked.

Jim was next and provided some comical relief with an ugly miss-hit that skirted along the ground, glanced off a tree, and landed in the high grass, only 100 yards from the tee. The barrage of taunts began. "Hey Jim, maybe you should switch to the ladies tee?" "Five bucks that Sam drives further." "No wonder all the snakes run for cover when you're on the course." Boys!

Much to Jim's dismay, I hit a good shot — coming to rest 140 yards on the left side of the fairway. It was a perfect lie for my next shot. Maybe I should play this game more often; I was actually having fun. I nearly skipped back to the cart. "Not bad, huh?" Looking for some praise.

"That was good … you slowed your stroke and kept your head down." Disappointed that Paul didn't show more enthusiasm for my improvement, I got a firsthand dose of what his direct reports feel.

Without missing a beat, Paul continued, "OK, I know that is one of my holes. I don't always listen, but I think I am good learner."

To keep it genuine, I asked, "Is it possible to learn if you don't listen? How can you truly understand and develop your people if you don't listen to them? And I mean listen deeply? How often are you really present? Meaning, how often do you really concentrate on what they are saying and feeling? I suspect most of the time when they are talking you are not really listening, you are thinking about what you are going to say. Even now, true?"

"I think I listen ... but you may have a point. I guess if I am going to be honest, my wife tells me all the time that I don't really listen to her. That is probably something I can work on."

"Also, in terms of learning and keeping current, when was the last time you took a leadership or business class or seminar that wasn't absolutely mandatory by the company?"

"It has been a while."

"When was the last time you took a golf clinic or watched a golf training video?" I was going for the juggler.

"Ouch. You probably heard that I take one week each year and attend a different golf school somewhere in the world. It combines a great week away with my golf passion. And yes I learn and retool my golf as well."

"I know you see the irony. I applaud you for your golf learning, but I also know that you are passionate about the work, yet you have a learning and a self-admitted listening 'hole.'"

Paul was marinating on that while I was chasing my ball down the fairway. After four strokes, I finally made the 306 yards to the green; however, given my route, I had probably traveled more than 500 yards. This sport may look easy, but I am here to tell you it is not.

"So, Sam I get what you are saying. If we use the green we are on right now as an example, there are two and probably many more leadership approaches we could employ. If we were a poorly functioning team, each person would examine his own situation, hit the ball, and achieve some sort of result. If we were a higher-functioning team with a leader who facilitated listening and learning, we would share the information we gathered about the hole; we would watch each person's putt and discuss how the subsequent golfers could learn and adjust. The expectation is that our overall results would be much better."

"It takes a strong, confident leader to facilitate listening and learning. And it requires engaging others and being willing to move off your own point. These are not necessarily easy things to do. In fact, I think that many businesses are beguiled by the authoritative leader, the person who takes charge, depends on his or her own knowledge and experience, and deals out orders."

"That sounds like a good thing," quizzed Paul.

"Taking charge is not a bad thing, but leaders must also be open to learning, listening and changing their opinion or direction. The most tragic example is the Space Shuttle Challenger. To help us learn in business, some very smart people created a team 'game' or exercise that uses the Challenger data disguised as a race-car situation. The teams get to decide given the data and business pressures whether to race or not. Although offered, few teams request additional data. And most, over 90 percent vote to race. Each team has to publicly proclaim their decision. After all teams have weighed in, it is divulged that they just blew up the Challenger killing all the astronauts. The teams are then given the data that they could have received if requested, which clearly indicates an impending disaster if they choose to race; the teams are asked to revote whether to race now given the new information. Here is the truly scary thing ... most teams stick by their original decision to race despite the fact that they know it will end in disaster. It is astonishing ... but it tells us a lot about human nature. Many don't listen or gather information or learn; and once they publicly proclaim their position, changing that position is almost impossible regardless of the circumstances. No wonder it takes a strong leader to listen, learn, engage and be willing to change one's position ... they are swimming against the tide of human behavior."

"That is frightening. I would like to believe I wouldn't fall into that trap. Yet, I know I have 'stuck to my guns' more times than I should have in the past. Fortunately, no tragic consequences like the Challenger.

"So if I am weak in this group of leadership funda-mentals, what can I do? You know I am focused on goals, I am impatient, and there is no way I am going to take the time to assemble everyone all the time to build a consensus."

"This is where you need to be thoughtful and practi-cal. You want to win ... however, to win, maybe you need to go slow to go fast to get to the right decision; 'walk the green together' so to speak to facilitate team learning. You won't always have the time. Some decisions require imme-diacy; but a large part of your responsibility is also helping others become better in their jobs. How can you do that if you don't listen, engage, understand their perspectives, and help them to learn from you and each other?"

We all finished off the hole relatively cleanly. As we picked up the flag and assorted clubs, Paul mulled over his thoughts. Cleaning off his putter as we stood by the back of the cart, he asked, "Any pointers on how to be present? How to listen and learn more effectively with my team?"

"I grant you this is hard. When it is not natural, it takes a lot of conscious effort to be present. It takes practice and hard work. To help you, first, try to control your rush to the answer. Given your fast pace and quick thinking, that will be a challenge. Yet, if you can keep yourself in the information gathering stage longer or what I call the 'fog state,' you will be much more open to asking questions, listening and learning. It will make you more present. Second, use that fog state to listen deeply to your people so you get a better understanding on how they think. In that way, you can not only gain a broader perspective, but you can also learn how to help them with their thinking. Which I might add is a key responsibility of a leader."

"That doesn't sound that hard."

"Trust me it is; particularly when you have proclaimed your answer or solution. Remember the Challenger example. In fact, for one executive I was coaching, we put a poster of the Challenger on his office wall. It was a constant and clear reminder to be present, ask questions, listen, and learn. Being quick, decisive and wrong is not a recipe for long-term success."

"That Challenger poster might be a good idea."

"Maybe you should get two — one for the office and one for your home."

"Ouch. Sam, did this coaching session turn into a marriage counseling session as well?"

"If the therapy couch fits, lie down on it. However, it is not a bad idea to practice at home. You are trying to adjust your behavior, to become more present. The more you practice the more it will become habitual. Try it tonight with your wife ... listen, learn, be present. You will be surprised at the response you get."

"I am always surprised at the response I get," laughed Paul.

"You just busted yourself. If you are always surprised, you are not learning. To quote Dr. Deming, 'Experience alone teaches us nothing.' Now with a theory and practice you might indeed learn how to get the response you want at work and at home. I promise to work with you on your 'adjustments' going forward."

"Well, it's worth a try," confided Paul.

I couldn't help but smile — being Paul wasn't easy, and I suspect being Paul's wife was no picnic. Yet, this was a major breakthrough. If Paul were willing to try and to adjust his behavior, we might actually be able to make some progress on his leadership effectiveness and ward off Frank's hatchet. No promises, but it was a start.

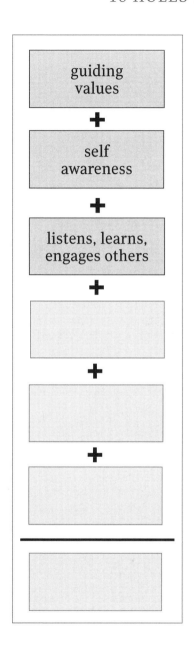

NO LEADER IS AN ISLAND

Surprisingly, Mario was preparing to tee off first, having "parred" and besting Paul by one stroke.

expanded network

"Paul, thanks for taking a dive on the last hole so that Mario could win one," teased Jim. "I am trying to sell him on a new software upgrade, and he will be much more receptive if he wins at least a few holes."

"Jim, you do know that I can hear you?" Mario teased back. "I didn't realize that you were trying to sell me. Of course, the brochures and ROI analysis that you have sitting in the cart might be a dead giveaway."

Paul shook his head, "You sales guys are all alike ... always nipping at our heels."

The 6th hole was a major challenge for me and took all my concentration and much-needed guidance from

Paul. It also was a good time to let some of the leadership fundamentals we had been talking about soak in a bit.

Curiosity getting the better of him, Paul questioned, "So how many more of these leadership holes are there? We've covered three so far — and we just finished the 5th hole. I just want to pace myself and make sure we stay in synch."

"Knowing your behavioral style, you're not going to like this ... there are three more fundamentals that you keep referring to as holes. So it is not a one-to-one correlation, which probably annoys you. You like things that are organized, structured and planned. Sorry ... think of it as a push on your comfort zone."

"You're right about that. I like things to be balanced and organized. There should be nine capacity elements and nine effectiveness elements to go back to your sand drawing of the six-square box. That would put everything in balance and synch with our game." Smiling and after a short pause, Paul continued, "However, in reflection, I should not be surprised. You already broke the four-square-box rule of consulting. So, it is not surprising that you screwed up the whole numbering thing as well."

"Leadership is not all clean and organized ... so it makes sense that my model reflects that; however, I do try to provide a clean and organized way to think about it. True?"

"The jury is still out. So what is next?"

"World-class leaders are not islands."

"That's it?"

"Yep."

"You mean that leaders should not be isolated."

"Exactly. One of the key ingredients for long-term success is building a strong and expanded network. I am talking in terms of external networks. Assuming that leaders follow the 'listen-and-learn' element, they will more naturally develop the internal network. Here I am talking about the importance of developing a connection outside of your business and even your industry. How big is your professional network?"

"Pretty good."

"With 24 years of business experience, your network should be very deep and very broad. Are you closely connected to your customers? Do you regularly meet with them? Do you have industry experts that you can call upon for ideas and advice? How about legal? Financial? Supply chain? Outsourcing? The deeper and broader your network, the greater your capacity to lead."

"Well, I can now add you to my network for leadership counsel."

"Absolutely. I am honored to be part of your network;

and I consider you part of mine. It is very sad to see leaders become isolated. I worked for a manager who had bullied his way into a leadership position. He was completely isolated. He intimidated everyone and depended upon his knowledge alone for everything. It was a very dysfunctional organization. He was a key influencer in the larger business and helped navigate the business into bankruptcy. His lack of perspective focused the company solely on profits and greed that ultimately led to the downfall of the organization. He had no network and listened to no one. His guidance caused the company to sacrifice its ethics which put the whole company at risk. The number of employees and families that lost their livelihoods is shameful."

"I think I know of whom you speak. The political world provides many examples as well. Richard Nixon is probably a prime example ... isolated, paranoid, distrusting." Paul added.

"Paul, your challenge is to develop that expanded network. As we spoke earlier, it is not your natural behavior to engage with others. So have Fran set up regular customer meetings to stay connected and utilize organizations that more match your style to meet and develop professional friendships."

"Such as?"

"Clearly, your country club is a start. There are many successful, professional people who are members. Seek them out. You don't need to ask them formally to be in your network, but you can build your own casual 'kitchen cabinet' so to speak; a casual lunch every few months or dinner, a call to ask an opinion. You will be surprised how open and willing people will be. Beyond the club, given your comfort zone, consider joining professional groups that provide deep relationships. Groups like Vistage, Renaissance Executive Forums, Alliance of CEOs, Young Presidents Club, etc., are a great way to build lifelong relationships and a strong professional network. And industry groups are also great, but you generally have to be very active or on the board to build strong relationships. I know you are more about what you know and do as opposed to whom you know, but your limited network is 'hole' for you. Don't let it blindside you."

"I hate to admit you might be right. I would appreciate if you would introduce me to one of those groups when I get back from my trip next month. I have been approached several times about joining such groups, but I never made it a priority. Maybe it is time I do? Or is it too late? I am getting a little 'long in the tooth' you know."

"Never too late ... plus, you will give as well as get."

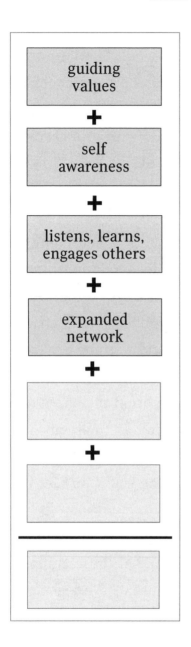

WHERE'S THE BEEF?

"Is there a lifeguard for this hole?" Mario asked. "That is definitely a large lake. Jim, how many balls have you donated to 'Nessie'?"

competency

"Too many. The 7th hole is rather infamous here at the club. Many are convinced that there is a large magnet that attracts golf balls to the lake ... you're right, sort of our own Loch Ness monster for golfers."

Golf is hard enough with all the bunkers, trees, out-of-bounds, changing topography, wind and weather, etc. Why on heaven's green earth do they need to add water hazards? That is just mean spirited. Oh well ... as I stand facing my teed-up ball, I am fully prepared to go for a swim. Naturally, Mario, Jim and Paul have all successfully avoided the water. With 165 yards to the hole, they are comfortably grouped together on the front of the green. I sense that all three have their fingers crossed for me; if not for supportive reasons, then at least to keep the pace of play going. Thankful that the women's tee was 125 yards, I selected and Paul agreed that I should use my 4 iron.

Paul encourages, "You have been striking the ball really well today, so don't even think about the water. Just relax. Keep your head down, and we will watch where it goes." He sounds just like my husband. I must look up even more than I realize.

With their hopeful eyes burning into me, I exhale, pull the club back and start my rotation. Please don't go into the water ... please, please, please.

What?! Worse than going into the water, I went nowhere. I whiffed it. I completely missed the ball. Anyone who plays golf knows that happens, but that doesn't make it any easier to accept. Even I had to laugh ... what else can you do?

"Did anyone see where it went?"

"Sam, hold on. Let me get my distance finder out of my bag so we can measure." Jim offered.

"OK, that was just a practice swing. I am glad I can provide some comic relief for all of you." With that, I lined up again, thankful that the women's tee was only

125 yards, exhaled, and hit a fair shot down the middle of the fairway. Nessie would have to wait a little longer for one of my bright fluorescent golf balls.

As we drove to my ball, Paul repeated the leadership fundamentals thus far. "Guiding values, self awareness, listen, learn, engage and expanded network — so what is next? I am starting to see how the pieces all hang together. Maybe you should turn it into a song? Like The *Twelve Days of Christmas.*" With that, Paul started singing the song with a new chorus: "big networks, deep engaging listener, high emotional intelligence, and a set of real guiding values."

"I think you may be onto something. Let's think big — how about a Leadership Opera?"

"Sort of like Tommy and The WHO?" added Paul.

"I think we are losing it. It only took seven holes for me to make you crazy."

"That may be true," agreed Paul. "But you can't beat fresh air, golf, and a good laugh."

"You are right about two of the three."

My second stroke landed my ball on the green only four feet from the hole. Paul congratulated me on my aim and execution. Early on he had suggested an adjustment to my grip, and, other than the whiff on my last tee shot, it seemed to be helping.

Riding to the green, I began the next fundamental. "What do you think is the next element?"

"Let me think. If I can get the *Twelve Days of Christmas* out of my head, I should be able to come up with something."

"Let me give you a hint. What if instead I was trying to coach your golf game? Would you listen or respect my suggestions? Would you follow my directions?"

"I would listen ... just like the third element − be present, listen, learn, engage."

"Well, you might, at least initially; but once you uncovered that I had no idea or was marginal at best, you would not follow my coaching. True?" Paul nodded agreement. "A leader has to be competent. Not in all things, but at least important core things. Another reason the leader needs to listen and engage, even more so in those areas he or she is not the resident expert."

"Very true," Paul concurred. "A leader must be competent. Remember John Sculley? Didn't he come from Pepsi and replace Steve Jobs as CEO of Apple back in the 1980s? I just remember a lot of turmoil emanating from Apple during that time. Sculley had grown up in Pepsi, married the CEO's daughter or step-daughter, ends up CEO of Pepsi, and then moves to Apple. It just always seemed to me that he was missing the core competency of technology and the fresh perspective one needed during that time. Creating and selling a new emerging technology like PCs in the 1980s was not the same as selling cans of soft drinks. Not that anyone had a great depth of competency at that point, but Sculley just seem ill-fitted."

"Jobs sure has shown his competency in running and growing technology companies, hasn't he? Both Pixar and Apple have done amazingly well. However, I suspect Jobs has a few other leadership holes. I don't know first-hand, but you hear a lot of comments about his style."

Finishing off the hole with reasonable putting, Paul brought up another CEO. "What about Nardelli? Robert Nardelli who went to Home Depot from GE and is now at Chrysler. Again, I think his downfall at Home Depot was his lack of retail competency. He grew up in manufacturing and distribution it seemed. What did he know about running a large consumer retail organization? What were they thinking?"

"My opinion is that Home Depot is just now recovering from all the mistakes and loss of customer focus made under Nardelli. What havoc can be created!" Paul said shaking his head.

"I don't know why, but it always brings to mind 'the where's the beef?' commercial. If you are missing the meat, a big fluffy bun is not going to going to compensate for the lack of beef. Your people will see through it ... if there is no 'beef,' no competency, they won't follow you, they won't respect you, and they will not be loyal. A leader must be competent in at least one or more of the core-needed competencies.

"And before you ask, I don't think that competency is one of your holes. You know the business from the ground up; you are very competent and highly respected for your knowledge."

"However, what I am gathering from you here today is that my competency might grow if I expanded my network and listened and learned more."

I was delighted with Paul's thoughtfulness and candor. "True. You are very competent, yet there is always more to learn. Learning from your team or external folks can only make you better."

We drove in silence to the 8th hole.

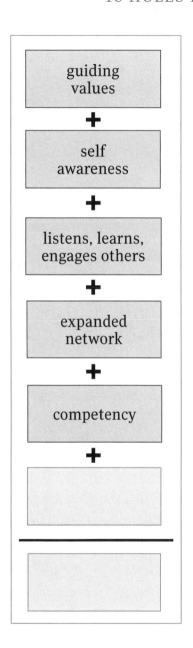

GOLFER, BAKER OR CANDLESTICK MAKER

I don't know about Paul, but I was mentally and physically exhausted by the 8th hole. Between

| courage and passion |

concentrating on golf and concentrating on Paul, I was beat. Plus, I was hitting a lot more balls than anyone else in our foursome, and probably anyone else on the course for that matter.

Without verbalizing it, we took a mental break from the leadership coaching and focused on having fun and playing golf. Paul was providing a lot of pointers, and it was building my confidence. My flubs were decreasing, and I was able to analyze what I was doing wrong when the ball didn't cooperate.

The 8th hole was actually fun and rejuvenated me.

Regardless, I was definitely ready for a lunch break, only one more hole to go.

The 9th hole was a daunting challenge — 527 yards with a steep, rocky gully in front and off the right of the tee and a lake that tightly fit into the crux of the dog-leg-left fairway. The only question was how many balls would be sacrificed? There was no way I was going to chase a ball into the gully. It was known to be a sanctuary for rattle snakes, spiders and other unsavory vermin. No golf ball was worth that. And clearly, the lake was already expecting a contribution from at least one of us.

"Ah, mulligan stew, Sam. Go ahead, take another one," offered Mario. With only one golf ball sacrificed to the gully, I made it across the deep ravine with my second shot."

From the tee, Paul drove us to the edge of the gully. He jumped out of the cart, skipped over several boulders, plunged his hand down a crevice next to a small scrub brush, and plucked out my ball — faster than you can say "antivenin."

Bounding back to the cart with a huge smile on his face, I was struck at how enthused he was about retrieving my snake-sacrificed ball. "Paul, I would never have gone after that ball. I can't believe you knew where it was and were willing to go get it. I certainly wouldn't want you to do anything that is unsafe." It was just a ball, but I have to say my respect for Paul just went up another notch.

"No worries. I am used to retrieving balls in the gully. I think my wife hits them in there on purpose." However, I couldn't help but notice a little more pride in his voice.

"Well this is a perfect segue to the last foundation element – courage and passion. Whether it is golf, business, or whatever, to be a leader, you must have courage and passion. They are tightly linked."

Slightly out of breath, Paul agreed, "You are right about that. I have worked for many, many bosses. Very few had courage and passion. Why would anyone want to work for a boss who doesn't have the passion for the work? And if you don't have the passion or care about the work, you most likely won't need courage, because you aren't impassioned to take risks."

"I work with a lot of companies, and it is always shocking to me when I find organizations that have little or no passion. You have to ask what has driven the passion out of the company? The leaders? The reward systems? What? Because, I always start with the assumption that someone started this company with a dream, purpose, and a burning desire to succeed. What drove it out?"

Paul's enthusiasm flared, "It doesn't take long to

recognize that those leaders who can create and sustain a culture of courage and passion for the business will win."

"Very true. Just compare two organizations — everything the same, except one is courageous and passionate about the work, the other is not. Which one do you think has a better chance to prevail? And which one would you rather be a part of?"

"I remember working for a Regional VP of Operations many years ago. The guy had completely checked out. He was unhappy and could care less about the business. He was like a wet blanket. I could almost feel him extinguishing my fire for the job. I bet he did a lot of damage."

"And shame on the leaders for allowing that to occur or causing it.

"Life is too short not to love what you are doing. Granted every day may not be a joy, but the majority should be. Leaders have to be passionate and courageous, but it is even more than that. Truly great leaders set the tone and infect passion and courage for the whole organization. Otherwise the company will slowly fill up with guys like your past Regional VP of Operations.

"Allow me to add that a critical part of that passion needs to be focused on helping your employees develop and be successful. I highly recommend you read Chip Conley's book, *Peak.* It is very insightful about the importance of creating a culture that promotes not just jobs or careers, but a calling. It is a milestone book in my opinion."

Working with many different companies, whether Mom and Pop operations or Global 100 conglomerates, I frequently come across owners or managers who complain that their people are not energized, not passionate about the work. Many are not even aware that the passion is missing. By walking around, it is easy to observe. One such client comes to mind. It was a large manufacturing operation — hundreds of employees. There was no joy, no passion in the work. Everyone seemed to wear a veil of boredom or numbness. The leaders were convinced that these low-wage earners had no passion ... that this was as good as it gets.

Yet, observing as the employees clocked out each afternoon, one could witness a transformation. The veils vanished and an energized, engaged person reemerged. It almost looked as though they were waking from a trance. They became animated, teasing each other, showing interest in family and friends. Many played league sports in the evening and poked fun at the latest losing team members. The passion was there, it just wasn't directed at the work. As a leader, you have to ask why not.

As we started to work with the company and with the leadership, we were able to bring that energy and passion into the operation ... productivity increased, quality issues decreased, worker complaints all but disappeared, revenues increased. It became a great place to work. Leaders must take a hard look at their operations. Are employees energized at work or only after work? If it is the latter, there is work to be done.

I continued, "And it makes no matter what the business is. I recently consulted for a large dog-food manufacturer. You could not believe the passion and courage of the team. Nothing was going to get in their way. Whether golfer, baker or candlestick maker, passion and courage are critical to success. Even dog food — passion makes you better."

"Sam you mentioned bakery. My wife was watching a show the other evening, 'Cake Man' or 'Cake Boss' or something. It was unbelievable. I sat down and watched it with her. The guy was amazing. What really came through was his passion for the business. It was infectious. He was so excited about cakes, and he had the courage to try anything. I don't know about any of the other leadership elements, but it was clear that this cake guy was full of passion and courage."

"I've seen it. And you're right, his passion and courage are so infectious that you want to join his team despite the family bickering. World-class leaders are passionate about the work, their customers, and their employees. Their focus is on helping both customers and employees thrive and succeed."

"Just think how energized and excited people can become about their jobs ... that can translate to increased productivity, innovation, more fulfilling lives, and profits. The leader is the foundation in igniting or creating that culture."

"Before you say anything, I know that may be one of my holes — at least in terms of creating a passionate and courageous culture. I think I have it myself, Sam. But I may not be creating it for others."

"I believe that is true. And I know your people have it in them to be passionate and courageous."

We were so engaged in the conversation, I hardly notice all the strokes I was taking. I avoided the lake, by skirting along the right side of the fairway as far away from the water as possible. Jim came close to losing one ball in the lake, but a clump of grass saved him.

Paul made par while Mario and Jim settled for one over par with six strokes. If I hadn't left one for the gully snakes, I would have been only two over par. Since we were playing casual golf, I was penalized one stroke for the gully ball. I guess in serious play, I would have been penalized more than that. My comrades were probably taking pity on me. How pathetic ... I really need to play more, but my passion was elsewhere.

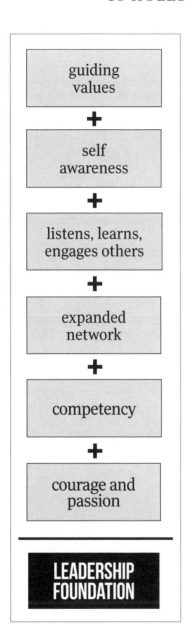

THE BACK NINE: DO YOU KNOW WHAT TO DO WITH IT?

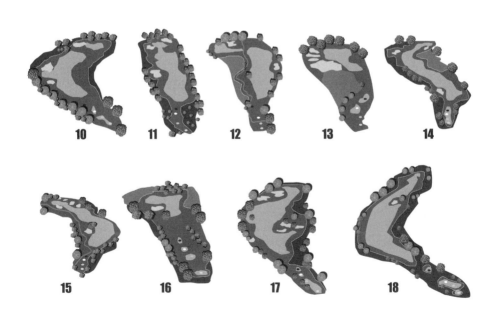

MAKING THE TURN

Paul couldn't drive the cart fast enough from the 9th hole to the café for my liking. With a rolling

right people in right jobs

stop, I jumped out. "Meet you at the grill in a minute," I tossed over my shoulder as I sprinted to the restroom. Nothing like a bathroom break to refresh you.

It was barely 11:00 a.m.; I had made it to the turn — only nine more holes to survive. Who decided on 18 holes anyway? Wouldn't 12 be much more reasonable? Play for a few hours, then run errands, get home in time to have a pleasant dinner. With 18 everything seems like a rush. Unless you start at sunrise, the entire day is consumed by golf; however, I doubt my male companions would see the logic of only 12 holes.

Proclaiming my hunger, I joined the others in studying

the menu. "Sam, what will you have? It is my treat." Stealing a couple of minutes, we settled into patio chairs to gobble down an abbreviated lunch.

Mario apologized, "I couldn't help but overhear parts of your conversation this morning. What were you saying about golf and leadership? I was only getting bits and pieces, but it sounded rather intriguing."

Paul jumped in, "Sam is providing me some leadership coaching. So, we thought we would get away from the office and the golf course sounded like a good idea. To take advantage of the day, she has been comparing leadership and golf."

"Sounds interesting. Would you mind if I listen in a bit? I promise not to get in your way." Mario asked.

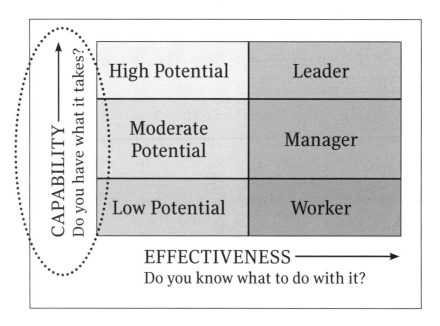

"Yeah, if you don't mind, we'd enjoy listening in." Jim added, wanting his client to have an enjoyable day with him on the golf course regardless of the topic of conversation ... and probably very thankful that he could still have his one-on-one time with Mario while riding in the cart.

Paul jokingly said, "Sure as long as Sam agrees not to triple charge us."

Glad that Paul seemed relaxed with the idea, I joined in, "My leadership coaching fees for the remaining nine holes will be: One, free golf pointers *from* each of you; two, freedom for me to pick up the ball and move on whenever I please; and, three, a well-deserved drink at the end of the day."

"Now you're talking. So, what have we missed so far?" Mario asked.

"Sam, let me show off and prove to you I really am listening, although help me if I get stuck." Using the back of a cocktail napkin, Paul drew the six-square box. "This is Sam's theory of leadership. And I have to say I am starting to see the wisdom in her buckets."

He explained the two "buckets" — the do-you-have-what-it-takes bucket and the do-you-know-what-to-do-with-it bucket. He shared how one is the foundation and the other determines effectiveness; how a leader must have a combination of both in order to achieve

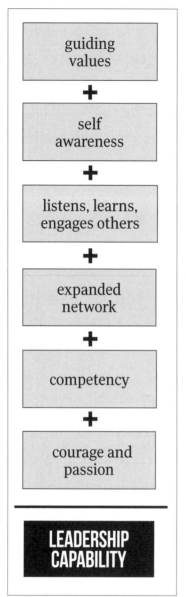

world-class leadership. Circling the capability axis, Paul continued. "This morning we have been talking about the capability factors or foundational elements. Sam, grab another napkin and draw the elements so I can show Mario and Jim. There is more substance here than just six boxes. And I have to say I am pleased that Sam has not 'dumbed it down' to four boxes. People *and leadership* are more complex than that."

I responded to the order and quickly drew the leadership foundation "equation" on another cocktail napkin.

I couldn't help but smile ... what a good student Paul was. At least he heard and understood — that alone was worth any humiliation I had to endure.

Mario was genuinely interested and asked a lot of questions. In response, Paul delved into each element, offering candid personal evaluations of himself. My smile got broader. Jim was also interested, but probably most pleased that his client was having a great day of golf and a great conversation.

"Paul, I am truly impressed. And Sam, I am curious about the back nine. You have piqued my interest."

"Great. One warning, however, I have a few cards up my sleeve for Paul. So, you can listen, but you must also participate. OK?"

"Sounds fair to me. What's next?"

Feeling the time pressure, Paul suggested we drive to the 10th tee and continue the conversation there.

Not everyone stopped for a lunch break, so a couple of groups jumped ahead of us at the turn. We were consequently forced to wait until the fairway was clear to tee off. Mario could not contain his curiosity, "What is the next element? And these are in the 'Effectiveness Bucket,' right?"

"Yes. Let me start with a question. Why do you carry so many clubs in your bag? Why don't you save money and just play with one club?" I asked.

Mario looked at me strangely, thought a moment and then turned to Paul, "This is her instruction method, right? OK. Well, each club has a different purpose. The woods are for long distances, the various irons for mid-range to short distances, and the putter is for the greens — it depends upon the angle and distance you need. Golf really is a game of geometry and skill."

"So, basically, each club has a particular purpose, a particular strength, right? And what you have done is assemble a collection of clubs that will help you in the various situations you may find yourself. If you are tee-ing off, or in the fairway, or heaven forbid in the sand trap, you pick the club that best fits the situation so that you can get the best score."

"Exactly," Jim responded, rolling his eyes and hop-ing that this conversation didn't remain so simplistic.

"In some respects, each of you has assembled a 'team of clubs' that has a variety of strengths that you can utilize in order to get the best score. Knowing Paul's behavior pattern, I would not be surprised to discover that you researched all the available, top-end clubs. You probably checked the Internet for information and recommendations; you may have talked to friends, the Club Pro or other members to hear their experiences or opinions; you probably read magazine articles com-paring club technology and performance; and you may have tried out demos to get a firsthand experience be-fore buying your clubs, irons, etc. True?"

"I hate to admit it, but you are right. It took me

several months to decide on my current set. Though, I did buy a new putter two weeks ago almost as an impulse."

"How is the putter working out?"

"Actually, I am not sure. It's not quite what I expected ... but I haven't given up yet. The jury is still out."

"Curious ... you may have spent more time researching and studying what is the right set of golf clubs to buy, putting aside the impulse putter, than most managers spend selecting new employees.

"So think about that for a minute. You spent a significant amount of time 'getting to know the club set' before you bought. You needed to know how it *would perform*, if it *would meet* your needs, would it help you improve your game ... and did the set provide a full complement of strengths. Now think of your team at work. How much time did or do you spend with them getting to know their strengths? How they *will perform?* And what is the best use of their strengths?

"If we think of the golf course as the business environment, then you can apply the same approach to your team of people as you do your 'team of clubs.' Given the business situation, who would be best for the task or position? Sometimes, we think of who has the experience, knowledge, interest or whatever. But, frequently, we pick people like ourselves ... someone who behaves or 'thinks' like us; someone with whom we are comfortable."

"What's wrong with that? Sounds like the perfect solution to me." Paul joked half seriously.

"That's fair. So, if executives hire people just like themselves, is that a good strategy? So let's do a little experiment. Are you up for a little fun and don't mind jeopardizing your score today?" All three heads bobbed hesitantly in the affirmative. "Great. So here's the deal. We are going to pretend that the driver in your bag represents you and all your business strengths. You will use only the driver for the entire hole. Got it? You can only use your driver for all your strokes."

"Well, this just got a little more exciting!" exclaimed Mario.

"I hope we are not breaking any PGA or Club rules," I added.

"I'm not sure, but we will be careful on the green." Paul responded.

Jim quizzed, "What is your reasoning?"

The purpose of the exercise is to illustrate how even your best person or club in this case, may not be the best person for every job. Ready to try it?"

"Sure, I'm game," said Mario with Jim concurring.

"You are great sports!" I was pleased that Jim and Mario wanted to join in the "fun." It would make the day easier for Paul. "I am delighted that you are willing victims; just keep in mind that the goal is to enlighten your leadership. So, let the back nine begin."

Jim's competitive nature came out, "This shouldn't be too hard. With 388 yards and a sharp dogleg right, I always use my driver on this hole anyway."

"I agree. I want the distance; I want to get over the trees and past the bunkers." Paul offered.

"Great. So right off the bat you are a perfect fit."

Paul's drive off the tee was nothing less than magical right up until the point it took a strange bounce and landed in a bunker 125 yards from the hole. Jim had equally bad luck hitting a tree and coming to rest in the deep rough on the right. Mario fared better with a clean stroke comfortably rolling to a stop in the middle of the fairway 100 yards from the hole. With two strokes, I was able to overtake Mario.

I thought to myself, if this doesn't drive the point home, nothing will.

Jim struggled in the grass. His driver was probably the worst club for the situation. Knowing that it was going to be ugly, Jim just hacked it 20 yards to the fairway in hopes of getting a decent lie.

Paul on the other hand was studying the bunker. Clearly, drivers and sand don't mix. After one failed attempt to hit out of the sand, Paul changed his strategy. The bunker was scooped high on the hole side and low on the tee side. Changing direction, he used his driver gently to stroke the ball in the direction of the tee and safely onto the fairway. Although he backtracked a few yards, he was at least out of trouble.

Jim was working on his third stroke, Paul on his fourth, and Mario on his second — I have to admit I was enjoying this more than I should have. Welcome to my world of golf.

The challenge now would be distance control. Jim was lucky with his next stroke and landed on the fringe; but both Paul and Mario ended up overshooting the green. An array of comments could be heard under their breaths — best that they were all unintelligible. After two more strokes, I was on the green. I was not taking my own challenge to play with just my driver. I had enough challenges just being on the course as it was.

Now it was indeed going to get interesting.

First up, Jim approached his shot trying to stroke as softly as he could while still getting some loft to place it near the flag. He overshot and was now in the bunker on the opposite side of the green.

Next was Paul. His lie was bad, sitting in a clump of high-cut grass. After a few practice swings, Paul made contact. The ball jumped out, hooked left, cruised past the flag, and ended up in the bunker next to Jim's ball.

"Beach party!" yelled Jim. "Bring the beer, we may be here awhile!"

All eyes turned to Mario who finessed it ... his light touch was perfect, the ball gently rolling within two feet of the hole. He couldn't contain his joy, doing a "Chi Chi Rodriguez," swashbuckling his club and sheathing it on his side like a sword, as he swaggered to the flag and waited for the rest of us.

Jim planted his feet in the sand and dug his driver gently into the ball. Much to everyone's surprise, it snaked out of the bunker, popped up, and bounced a few feet away from the hole.

Laughing in disbelief, Mario couldn't help himself, "Well, even a blind squirrel finds a nut every once in awhile!"

"What?! That is pure talent. I analyzed the shot, compensated for the driver, made all the necessary adjustments. I am quite offended." Jim teased.

As the self-appointed boss for the foursome, I said "OK, before the course marshal comes after us, you can have one more shot with your driver. Then use whatever to finish out the hole."

Not to be undone, Paul with deep concentration

gently guided his ball out of the bunker and onto the green leaving him a 20-foot putt. His relief evident – the hole was insight.

The three egos were unyielding; despite my offer, all three stuck with their drivers to complete the hole. A few more putts, we were done with the 10th hole. Laughing as he replaced the flagstick, Mario confessed that he had always wanted to try an experiment like that.

Hiking back to the carts, everyone was having a good laugh. "OK, Sam you made your point. First, different jobs require different strengths. And second, just because I am the boss doesn't mean I can do everything great; but, if you tell my wife I admitted that, I will deny it." Paul joked.

"You know Sam, you made a very good point earlier. Some of us probably do spend more time selecting our golf clubs than we do selecting a key hire. Strange, huh?" Mario pondered.

BUT WAIT THERE'S MORE

Moving quickly to the 11th tee, we all made decent tee shots as we continued the discussion. "The fact

| right people in right jobs |

that many of us spend more time researching and selecting our golf clubs than we do getting to know and hiring our employees may sound ridiculous; but for me, in all honesty, it may be true." Paul confessed. "I spent a ton of time reading, thinking and testing clubs before I bought these clubs. However, when I hired my latest VP of Supply Chain, I read his resume, had HR check references, which as you all know is a pretty useless exercise nowadays, and ran him through about five interviews. My total face time with him, before we made an offer, was maybe three hours."

"I hate to admit it," Mario joined in, "but you're probably right. We try to make the best people decisions we can, but most of the time I feel as though I am blind-folded and gagged."

"It does feel like 'a crap shoot' most of the time. When I hire a new salesperson, it's a 50/50 chance that he will work out." Jim backpedaled, "Sorry ... or she."

"So why is that? We tout that our people are our most important asset, yet we are not good at selecting them, developing them, or promoting them. If we really knew what turnover or poor hires were costing us, we would have to fire ourselves. So, why after years and years of hiring and promoting people that we as managers are still so poor at it? Or is this as good as it gets? What do you think?" I asked.

"Ah. Good question. We certainly have made many productivity gains in supply chain, category management, customer relationship management, etc., but, you're right, we really haven't made any quantum leaps in hiring. The process really hasn't changed much from the 1950s other than the resumes are written with word processors, the application process is electronic with no or little human interaction, and we can Google people to find out what embarrassing information is available on the Internet. Other than that, not much else has happened."

"Being in the technology world, we certainly have

made some major strides in automation of the HR function with SAP and Oracle and more so with talent management programs like Taleo and MrTed," Jim added.

"I think Sam's point is the process. We may have automated the process, but the process itself is still the same — we just do 'poor' faster and more efficiently."

"I am sure that some HR managers would disagree with us, but from my perspective as the hiring manager, I think you're right ... not much, if anything has really changed. Basically, we post an open position with some obscure description of responsibilities; we then try to sort through the pile of applicants. For the 'lucky few,' we interview them trying to ask some trick questions to see into their inner souls — what do they really think? How will they really behave? Can they really perform the job? Or are they going to turn out to be my next big nightmare?"

Not needing to drive the point home further, everyone returned to playing with his full selection of clubs. By the time we got to the green, I thought the topic would have changed to golf again. Instead all three were still bemoaning the challenges of hiring the right people.

"If you think about it, in general, we hire for the *future* based on their *past* — or as best we can 'see' into their past. Once we believe that they have the right intelligence, education, experience and interest, then we cross our fingers and hope that they will perform in the job — that they will behave as we expect ... that if we need someone who is very detailed and strictly follows through, that she or he will actually do that."

Jim jumped in, "I have a great example: two years ago I hired a 'great salesman.' I had known him for years, smart, likable, interviewed great, been in the industry for 20 years, everyone knew him, great guy. I just knew he would be a star. Instead, he was a disaster. He never picked up the phone, never left the office to make a customer call, nothing. He spent the first three months in his office reading all the technical manuals. When I included him in client meetings, he would either recite the technical stuff or question whether we could do something I was suggesting to the customer. He never tried to understand the customers' needs or show empathy for their situations. What a mess! I had to let him go. After his salary, training, our time, lost business opportunities, I bet it cost us well over $250,000 for that one mistake; but given our process, I would make the same mistake again today. He appeared to have everything. And we even felt like we knew him. It sure wasn't a pleasant experience for either of us."

Everyone finished off the hole and started walking back to the carts. "But here is the frustration ... we're limited to what we can ask in an interview, what information we can gather on a candidate, and we can't take months getting to know the person," Mario countered.

"I agree it is frustrating to have such a critical process not provide the results companies need. And clearly some companies are more effective at it than others; but even with better methods like behavioral interviewing, our batting average is not very good." Paraphrasing a quote from Peter Drucker, I tried to do justice from what he wrote in 1985:

> *"Executives spend more time on managing people and making people decisions than on anything else – and they should. No other decisions are so long lasting in their consequences or so difficult to un-make. And yet, by and large, executives make poor promotion and staffing decisions. By all accounts, their batting average is no better than .333: at most one-third of such decisions turn out right; one-third are minimally effective; and one-third are outright failures. In no other area of management would we put up with such miserable performance."*

"A .333 batting average is darn good for baseball, but not for hiring or promoting. It is damaging to the employee, and it is costly in time, money and customer satisfaction. Think if we consider one round of golf as one business cycle. At the end of each round, you determined that you needed to get rid of one third of your golf clubs. You then had to spend time researching and finding their replacements, purchasing them, and then getting used to them. The cost would be enormous and you would be constantly breaking in new clubs that would most likely be reflected in higher golf scores ... or for business lower profits."

"I don't think that even I could justify playing with that expense ... green fees, club dues, are bad enough." Mario said.

"Oh I don't know. I understand that Jim's current budget for golf balls is probably that much already. In fact, we are all surprised that he can afford to play even now. Jim, didn't the course manager offer to hitch a trailer full of golf balls to your cart so you could make it through a full round of 18 holes?" Turning to Mario, Paul winked, "We don't call him water boy for nothing."

Jim being a good sport, roared with laughter, "OK, OK, so I like the water. I grew up near the Jersey Shore. What do you expect?"

Trying to summarize, "So, with respect to business, gentlemen, what I am suggesting are several things: One, leaders need to be deeply involved in selecting and hiring employees; it is so critical and cannot be handed off to HR alone; two, leaders need to be aware that there are analytics out there that can identify what strengths or behaviors are needed for a position and that can identify who has those strengths to perform the job — so you can set employees up for success before you even hire them; and, three, yes, spending more time with candidates is always better if possible, but applying predictive analytics and using them appropriately can actually take your batting average from .333 to .900 or better with little or no extra time. Where else can you get nearly a 300-percent improvement in a business practice?"

Mario asked, "Really? That sounds too good to be true."

After teeing off the 12th, I continued. "Not really. Many companies employ these tools and have for many years. They may just not want to share them; maybe they see them as a competitive weapon. It would be the same if you found a new golf ball that always flew straight and 50 yards further regardless of your stroke. If you were a competitive golfer, you wouldn't share the news about it would you? Bottom-line, there are a handful of quality tools and programs that could be used by any of your companies. And unless you invite your HR folks to be strategic partners at the table with you, they may not feel empowered or enabled to provide training for the top executives or to introduce new approaches for the benefit of operations, etc. And when I say new, I mean to your company. The analytics that I am thinking about have been used and regularly validated for decades."

Mario continued, "Then why haven't I heard about them?"

"I can't answer that." I responded

Paul jumped in, "Sam, one of the tools you are alluding to is the one you gave me and then debriefed me, right? Well, let me just say gentlemen, it 'nailed me.' In a very short time, Sam knew exactly my leadership style, my communication style, and my delegation style. It was almost eerie how she knew exactly how I would behave or as she said, 'My natural styles and strengths.' To have this information during the selection process would be incredible. It would be helpful in so many ways, not the least of which would be matching the person with the right strengths to the right job. Anything that would minimize having to fire an employee would be worth its weight in gold. It is painful and costly for all parties involved."

"So true," chimed in Mario. "Sam, I think we need to talk later."

On the fairway, we all focused on the game. No one was in serious trouble; but I was definitely getting tired of making so many strokes. I was undeniably working harder than the others.

Once we were on the green, I decided to add, "Another point I should address, depending upon your organizational responsibilities, is that you may or may not need a large complement of strengths on your team. By way of the golf analogy, if you only play the greens, you may only need a couple of putters (or strengths); same as if you are a functional manager, such as a call center manager. If that manager is only responsible for all inbound sales calls, he or she may need a lot of people all with the same profile or strengths. In golf terms, I just need putters, but a lot of them. Make sense?"

"I get it. Whereas, someone who plays the whole course or translated to business an enterprise manager who is responsible for multiple functions or the entire company, he may need to have a very large bag of clubs with a variety of strengths. For example, Mario probably needs a whole host of strengths on his team — he needs programmers, business analysts, system operators, customer service, etc. Each position requires a different set of knowledge and strengths. Consequently, since he has a variety of jobs on his team, he needs a variety of different 'clubs' in his bag ... employees who have the right knowledge, training, strengths for the specific job; but my regional sales managers are basically selling the same services to the similar client profiles, they need the people with the right strengths do that. And you're saying that we should know what that profile is and hire it. Otherwise, we are putting people into positions that set them up for failure. Right?"

"Bingo!" Impressed that Jim was so engaged, I gave him the thumbs up.

"Yes, I never thought of it in quite that way," said Mario. "I am most curious to know how you determine what you need beyond their experience and education. And how do you know a person matches what you need even before you hire him or her? Another question — won't this limit the diversity in the organization? Hopefully you will enlighten us by the 18th hole."

"Well, I am not sure how much more we will be able to cover on that topic today. Other than to say that there are approaches and tools that quickly and accurately identify needed job strengths. And briefly to answer your last question, these analytical tools actually increase the diversity."

Mario, with a bit more seriousness in his voice, "If there are methods that can help us as you say, then I definitely want to talk with you next week. OK?"

"Absolutely, give me your card later and I will call

you." Today was turning out better than I had hoped. I was afraid I might lose a client, not gain one. Heading toward the 13th, I was feeling pretty good.

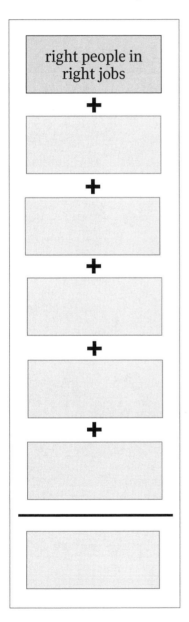

NANCY L. CLARK

DON'T EXPECT GREAT RESULTS IF YOU PLAY IN THE FOG

Overjoyed at reaching the 13th tee, I was definitely in countdown mode. Yippee, after this hole only five more to go.

create shared vision

"Sam, what's next? And remember, I have a tournament tomorrow ... the deal is not to ruin my game today," Paul reminded.

"Paul, you are so solid, it would take a lot more than these exercises to harm your game tomorrow." Jim offered a compliment.

Lined up by the carts and gazing at me expectantly, all three eagerly awaited the next challenge.

"Have you ever played golf in the fog?" I asked.

"Sure ... if it isn't too bad."

"Exactly, if it isn't too thick; but what if it is so bad you really can't see more that a few yards in front of you? What then?"

"When it gets that bad, there is no point in playing. You wouldn't know where the ball lands; you wouldn't even know what direction to hit the ball."

"You're right; it would be pretty pointless. However, I have another challenge for you. We are going to play this hole in the fog." I waited to watch their responses.

"How are you going to do that? It is a beautiful day, not a cloud in sight." Paul perplexed.

Baffled, Jim agreed, "This I have got to see."

"I don't know fellas. I am learning not to underestimate Sam." Mario's dark, thick right eyebrow quizzically rose.

"I just happen to have an eye mask with me, or you can use your golf towel."

Paul chuckled, "Just happened to have?" Convinced that I had premeditated the exercise.

"Fortunately, no one is close by. So, everyone get whatever club you plan to use and meet me on the tee."

This exercise may indeed put them over the edge, but at least I was having fun. With everyone on the tee,

I gave them the instructions. When it was their turn, they would put on the eye mask or towel — whatever they preferred. I would tee up their ball, then direct them where to place their club, and strike the ball. No one else could coach or provide hints. Amazingly, all three participated without complaint. I am not sure that I would have been so accommodating.

Not following the prescribed order, I suggested Mario go first. He obliged, handed me his tee and ball, and put on the eye mask. I placed his tee and balanced the ball on it. Then I guided him by placing his club in the proper position. He took a strong stance, pulled back his club, and just barely connected with the ball. It skidded forward about 40 yards off to the right (thankfully avoiding the water hazard) and clearly a few degrees off the line to the hole.

Mario yanked off the eye mask curious to see where it had gone, "Where did it go?"

"Not too far," Jim pointed.

"I hope there is a good reason for this exercise, Sam. If the point is hiring disabled workers, I get it. We can move on," Paul goaded.

"I promise; the point soon will be clear." I called Jim up next to hit, which resulted in basically the same result as Mario's hit.

Feeling relieved that he wasn't alone, Mario teased Jim, "Don't assume that making me feel better guarantees you a software sale."

Paul was next. Taking more time, requesting reassurance from me that the club was lined up properly, concentrating, he pulled back and swung. Not to be outdone, Paul took a big swing, striking under the ball, launching it straight up into the air.

Ripping off the eye mask, Paul searched "Where did it go?"

Returning to earth a few seconds after Paul removed his eye mask, the ball landed 50 yards from the tee, rolled a few feet, and nestled up against the edge of the lake. "You're lucky you missed the water. Too bad, I would be happy to abdicate my position as 'Club Water Boy,'" said Jim clearly enjoying that Paul hadn't hit it out of the park.

Being a good sport, Paul shook his head, "Well, I guess it could have been worse." Turning to me, "OK, Sam what is the deal? Other than goofing with us, why blindfold us?"

"Before I answer, let me ask how you felt doing this little exercise. Other than foolish, share your thoughts."

Jim spoke up first, "I felt very uneasy. I did not feel confident, and I did not want to embarrass myself with a poor stroke — which I clearly did."

Mario went a little deeper, "I felt frustrated. I wanted to avoid the water and get on the green. The distance to the hole is only 170 yards and very doable, but being blindfolded or playing in the fog as you say just made it confusing. I was interested in the exercise, but my interest or desire in the game diminished."

"Paul, what about you?"

"I felt the same as Mario — and probably a little more competitive with them as opposed to competitive with myself."

"Please explain that a little more."

"Well, after putting on the eye mask, it was obvious that reaching or knowing the hole location was not clear. Consequently, if my goal is to improve my game, but the game is no longer clear then at a minimum I wanted to do better than Jim and Mario. So my competitive focus changed."

"Interesting and very insightful." Pleased with Paul's candid reflection, I conjectured, "Had we really been playing in a dense fog, you may have considered success hitting the ball further than Mario and Jim even if it were in the wrong direction of the hole. Since you didn't know where the hole was, your only measure was where their balls landed."

After I hit from the lady's tee, we drove the 40 yards to Mario and Jim's balls. "I won't ask you to do the exercise again; but just think about how difficult it is when you aren't sure where the goal is." After a long pause, I continued, "Now consider how employees feel when they work in the fog. They are not sure what the goal is; they don't know how they are doing — or if they are headed in the right direction. Like Paul, they may decide to measure themselves against each other — which may explain in part why we have divisiveness and silos in many organizations. I propose that without a shared vision or goal we compete against each other, with a shared vision we compete together."

I couldn't tell if that was resonating or if they thought I was nuts. Everyone quietly made it to the green in one stroke, even Paul as he balanced against the edge of the lake. The putting was uneventful. Despite the poor start, Mario and I bogeyed the hole, Jim and Paul made par.

On the 14th tee, Mario was the first to speak. "I hate to admit that as part of the Bank's leadership team, I sometimes feel unsure of our direction. Even at my level, I guess the fog can play havoc."

"If you consider that most, if not all, of your employees are making business decisions every day, what impact does that have on results if they are not sure where the organization is headed? They may be making the best decision given what they know, but it may head the organization or team in the wrong direction. In lean times, poor decisions are even more painful."

Paul jumped in, "But what if like Mario, the leadership is not sure."

Boomeranging it back, "What do you think?"

"I think that is why they get paid the big bucks. If they don't know, they better find some people who can figure it out or they should step aside. A ship without a rudder is at the mercy of the current or worse the storm."

"I couldn't have said it better." Delighted with the conversation, I continued to push once we all reached the green, "Let me say that I don't think it is the CEO's sole responsibility to create the vision alone. She or he should involve the leadership team, key stakeholders, thought leaders, etc. Nothing is more useless than a vision or plan that never gets implemented. And unless people co-create the plan, own it, truly buy-into it, it will never be fully implemented. That is why it is so critical to engage a large group in the planning process and to cascade it throughout the organization so that it can be expanded, refined and owned. Otherwise, the leadership will spend all their energy trying to sell it. The CEO should instead own the responsibility of facilitating the process and providing input into the plan."

Walking to the green after moving the carts, Mario questioned, "Given what you just said a few moments ago, Sam, is that why getting the right people into the right positions is the first step? Because you want and need those people to help craft the vision?"

"Exactly. The CEO or boss probably has a fair idea of what the vision is. Then get the people on the team and really design it together with full input and ownership."

"You talked about cascading it. What did you mean?" Jim asked.

"Not unlike your sales planning. Engage each level in the process. It may need to go up and down the organization a few times, refining, improving, etc."

"I don't know if I follow. If the leadership team creates a vision, and then my sales team creates a vision, they might be in conflict."

"Oh, I see the confusion. The leadership team creates the enterprise vision — big and all encompassing. Then you would take that vision to the sales and marketing organization — get their input and ideas for improvement. Next you would challenge your sales and marketing leadership team to craft the sales and marketing vision. It would need to support and align with the enterprise vision."

"Thanks. That makes sense now."

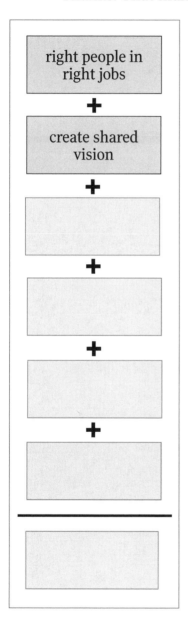

TALK IS NOT CHEAP

Despite the challenges I had thrown at Paul, he was only seven over par after the 14th hole, which

communicate

is a real testament to his golfing abilities.

Waiting quietly for the 15th fairway to clear, Paul spoke maybe more to himself than to me. "I need to work with Frank to make sure we have a clear enterprise vision. It should be lofty and challenging. And then I do need to involve my team more in creating our operational vision that aligns and supports achieving the enterprise vision. I guess that is where some of the foundational elements come into play as well — I need to listen, learn and engage my team. Actually, I guess all the fundamentals come into play." Not realizing that he kept it, Paul surprised me by pulling out the napkin with the "front nine bucket equation" that we shared at the break. He reviewed the six elements and how each one plays a part.

"Paul, I just have to say that moments like this make my job worthwhile. Your willingness to think deeply about your leadership style and how to adjust it is outstanding. I really appreciate your openness."

"Well, not to get all sappy here Sam, but I do appreciate your help. Frank and I are or were heading toward a collision. Something needs to change. And I now see that there are some things I need to do differently. I understand a little more why I piss him off. As you say, I don't want to make mistakes. So instead of brainstorming with him, I shut him down as to why we can't do something. I will try and go with the flow a little more. Not that it will be easy, but at least I understand more of our differences. I will consciously try and adjust ... as you so adeptly put it."

Quickly changing demeanor, Paul called us to attention, "OK, looks like we're up."

Taking control, I began, "For this hole, we are going to use Mario and me as guinea pigs, if that is acceptable to you?" Turning to Mario, he returned an affirmative grin. "Great. The reason we are using the two of us is because we are the least familiar with this course. Like a new or poorly led employee, we don't know the vision or plan for this hole; or any of the nuances that experience teaches after playing the hole multiple times. Now, with Jim and Paul acting as our bosses and course experts, you are going to assist us to achieve the best result for this hole. We will not look at the golf card or any signage; we will only depend on you to guide and communicate to us what and how to play the hole. Got it?"

"And the point is ...?" Jim asked.

"Communicate, communicate, communicate — talk is not cheap, it is necessary for us to do well. You and Paul need to confer with each other and then give guidance and direction to us. We need to hear one voice, no mixed messages on what to do, and how best to play the shot. If you and Paul communicate clearly and consistently, Mario and I should do well on the hole relative to our different skill levels."

"Now I'm feeling like the guinea pig." Jim jokingly admitted.

"I suggest that Jim and Paul tee off first — and that they explain everything they are doing and why so that Sam and I can understand and learn," said Mario jumping right into the fray.

Bowing slightly, Paul invited Jim to hit first. With great aplomb, Jim placed his tee on the far right side of the tee box, explaining that he needed to get a good angle to avoid the trees and bunkers on the left side of the fairway. Sounding like a professor, Jim lectured that the 15th hole could be challenging; a 386-yard hole with strategically placed bunkers that could cause you to over shoot and send you into the trees. He cautioned us not to over think it and to aim for the widest part of the fairway. Recommending we use a driver for distance, as long as we hit fairly straight, he confirmed there were no major obstacles we needed to go over. With that, he approached the ball and swung, the ball landing exactly as planned. Pleased with himself, he returned the bow to Paul and gestured him to take command of the tee.

Next up, Paul placed his tee close to Jim's spot. He agreed with Jim's analysis and recommendation. Adding that depending upon the weather, he may change his angle and go for a longer distance. Blasting the ball 240 yards, it rolled to the right side of the fairway, leaving him a perfect second shot. Asking if we had any questions or need for further clarification, he stepped aside for Mario.

Placing his tee near the other two, Mario stretched his arms over his head and twisted his torso to relax and prepare. Placing the club head next to the ball, Mario asked "his boss" to check his line. Paul and Jim, having a bit of fun, conferred and realigned him straight into the trees. Thinking better of it, they guided him to the proper angle and encouraged him to swing. To the relief of Jim, Mario hit a solid shot, straight up the middle and close to Jim's ball.

"I like all this support. That felt like my best shot of the day." Winking at me, "Sam, maybe there is something to this communication thing."

Moving to the lady's tee, everyone grouped around me. I felt like a golf diva with her entourage. With direction and guidance from Jim and Paul, I placed my tee on the right center of the tee box, lined up the shot, and swung. Excited to see where the ball went, I must have looked up too soon. Expecting to be near the others, I was disappointed to see my ball lazily bounce down the cart path on the left side of the fairway, finally rolling to rest in the rough near the trees.

Laughing out loud, I said, "Well, so much for proving the point on communication."

Joining in the humor, Paul offered, "Maybe this just reinforces your earlier point — get the right people into the right jobs. Vision and communication can only do so much."

"Touché. And thank you for the excuse. Yes, that is exactly the point I am making."

To save time, we retrieved my ball and caught up

with the others. Mario was preparing for his second shot. Paul jumped out of the cart to confer with Jim and to provide some coaching. They suggested to Mario that his 5 wood might be best given the distance, etc. Mario accepted their suggestion and lined up his club. Again, a beautiful swing, and the ball soared cleanly down the fairway and rolled onto the front of the green. Pleased again with his result, Mario thanked his communicators by bumping fists all around.

After Jim and Paul each explained their second-shot situations and strategies, each performed as expected. My strategy was simple: take a ball drop and hit the sucker. Who knew? My strategy worked this time.

Once all of us were on the green, communication increased significantly. Reading the green is both an art and a science. It was also fascinating to hear both Jim and Paul discuss the angles, dips, grain and speed considerations. They both offered to go first in order to provide Mario and me a better indication of how the green would play. I finished off with two putts, leaving Mario the green and his coaches to steer him to success. Like two mother hens, Jim and Paul circled the green. I bet they put more thought and effort into that putt than they did their wives' last birthdays ... I really shouldn't think such generalizations.

Lined up, head down, upper body lightly swinging like a pendulum, Mario shouted "Y-E-S!" as he watched his 20-foot putt roll, dip and ultimately fall into the hole. It was his first birdie on the back nine and only his third one of the day.

After the traditional high-five celebration, we joyfully regrouped at the carts to return our putters to their rightful bags and to prepare for the next hole. Both pleased and relieved that Mario did well, Jim asked Mario what he thought about the exercise.

"Clearly, it helped my game. I haven't played this course in several years, so having you both communicate and share your expertise made a big difference. Normally, you look at the golf card, check out the fairway, and then guess. However, in a broader sense and what Sam is underscoring, I think are several things: One, if we as leaders don't communicate, how will our team know what is happening, and what is the challenge or priority? How will they benefit from our knowledge and expertise? How will they know that we still are focused on the goal or plan? And second, I have to say that with Paul and Jim communicating and guiding me, I felt much more secure or confident. I am sure our employees, especially new ones who 'haven't played this course before' feel alone or isolated. The more we can do to assist them, provide clear expectations and goals, the better. Right Sam?"

"As long as you have the right person in the right job," I added which solicited an uncontained belly laugh from Paul. "On a serious note, as leaders you have to communicate. And communication takes all forms — written, oral, and most importantly through actions. If you say one thing, and then act another way you send mixed messages; but the key here is communicate regularly, clearly and consistently. You may get bored saying the same thing over and over again, but people need to hear it and need to trust what you say. Again, you see how communication is built on the foundation elements of values, listening, competency, passion, etc."

Jim quipped, "Paul, I don't think you are paying Sam enough."

"Hold on a minute ... I may be using her soon." Mario interjected.

"Oops. Sorry Sam."

Driving the cart to the next hole, Paul confided that communication was probably another hole of his.

"I agree, Paul. I think that is an area that needs some work. Knowing your profile, I suspect that you are so focused on the work and so busy, that you deluge your team with cryptic emails even late at night when you finally get time. With little encouragement for face-to-face interaction, your team may be confused and have trouble sorting out the real purpose or goal of what you want them to do. Consequently, I would not be surprised if you are frequently disappointed by members of your team because they don't meet your expectations, which is unfair because you have not been clear and/or have not encouraged them to meet with you to gain clarity."

"I hate to admit you may be correct," Paul confessed. "But a couple of my guys are great. They almost always get what I need."

"My guess is that they either have worked for you a long time and read you like a book and/or they depend upon each other to figure out what you want."

"Well, you're right about that. But isn't that a good thing?"

"It is a good thing, but it can also drive you to work with or favor only a couple of your people. As a leader you want to understand and leverage all your people. If you don't use all communication methods, you are probably sub-optimizing your resources."

"Well, it is something I will work on — another thing to add to a growing list."

"I hope you are not feeling overwhelmed, Paul. You have great strengths and are very competent. I am here to help you make those 'adjustments' until they become second nature to you."

"Good ... I think I'll need a lot of coaching for awhile."

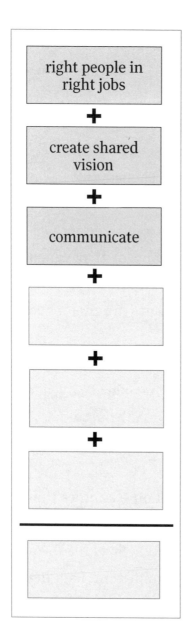

CHIROPRACTOR OR QUACK

The 16th was a gentle uphill, 156-yard hole, par three. Other than the lake to the right side of

align the right incentives

the green, the only other obstacle was a large bunker on the left front. I was getting tired of going to the lady's tee by myself, so I decided to tee from the men's; 156 yards was not so bad.

After everyone hit their tee shots, Jim was eager to continue, "Sam, what's next in your leadership bucket?"

"Well let me see — we have covered job fit, vision, communication, ummm ... the next is incentives: making sure that leaders align the right rewards. Or as I like to say, a leader has to be an organizational chiropractor to make sure everything lines up properly."

Jim nodded and agreed, "It can get complicated in

sales; but basically, the key is to figure out the right base and commission structure."

"You're right it can get complicated. The important thing is to think first about what behavior you want to encourage. Staying with sales, you probably want a buffet of incentives that encourage your team to get new clients, expand or cross-sell existing clients, provide outstanding customer service, introduce new products or services, maintain margins, team sell for national or global accounts, whatever."

"That's a great list, Sam. Maybe I could use your help too," Jim smiled.

"Those are fairly easy to address when we are just talking about financial rewards. Yet many leaders run into problems because their incentives shift or become too focused."

"What do you mean?" Paul inquired.

"I am sure you've seen it a lot. A company launches a big incentive program to go get new clients. If I am a sales person, I hear the message loud and clear — new clients equals more money. All the sales people run around chasing new clients. New client business increases — great. However, existing clients are neglected, existing sales drop. Another new incentive program is launched — grow existing client sales. And again the sales people receive that message and focus their time and attention on existing clients. Existing client sales increase, new clients decrease."

"It is a bit like that gopher game ... wherever the head pops up, bop it down," Mario added.

"So the financial incentives have to be well thought out and should be considered holistically. As I like to say, every company is perfectly aligned to get the results it gets. If it wants different results, it needs to adjust its alignment. Hence the need for leaders also to be organizational chiropractors; but that is just the financial portion and compensation could include cash bonuses, trips, cars, whatever. Another important incentive is how and when you recognize performance."

Now confused Jim asked, "I don't follow you."

"It goes back to self awareness and truly understanding others. I will explain on the green."

Paul and I drove to my ball so I could chip onto the green. With that successfully accomplished, we joined Mario and Jim as Paul pulled the flagstick.

All three had a chance for birdie, so the incentive discussion was on hold for a few minutes. However, I was delighted that the previous "communication" was flowing over to this hole. Jim and Paul were openly discussing the angles and speed and offering advice to all. Until the last hole, advice on how to play green had been limited at best — other than a few pointers Paul had given me.

Both Mario and Paul birdied; Jim's ball hit the rim and refused to go in. And I was more than satisfied with my two putts. Mario replaced the flagstick and encouraged the incentive discussion to resume.

"Maybe the best way to explain it is to share an example from one of my clients who will remain anonymous. It was several years ago. Let's call him Kirk. Kirk is the EVP of Sales for a large pharmaceutical company. Now Kirk is a high-energy, extrovert — very persuasive, incredibly outgoing, just a huge personality. When he walks into a room, you can't help but feel his energy and presence. A couple of times a year, he brings all his sales people together for a big meeting. And given his profile, he loves hosting big events — and he loves being on stage. Every minute of the three-day meeting is planned and action packed. Prizes are given and over the course of the meeting, the top performers in various categories are invited onto the stage in front of some 800 people. Many of the top performers are invited to say a few words or are asked to lead sections of the meeting. It is a huge extravaganza. So, how do you think these meetings are received?"

"Probably great," Jim was quick to respond.

Paul jumped into the cart and suggested, "Let's get to

the 17th, it looks like it will be clear in a minute; we can continue there." With that, we all made our way to the next hole.

At the 17th, I saw that Mario was eager to continue the conversation. Turning to Jim, I directed my comments first to him, "After a few holes of golf, I believe your profile may be similar to Kirk's. You are probably great on stage and enjoy the whole camaraderie of 800 people. Yet as I started to work with Kirk's regional and district managers, we uncovered that the top performers were very unhappy. They were completely different profiles from Kirk. The top performers were technical and reserved. They were not socially focused and found these meetings more punitive than rewarding. They hated being on stage and probably felt physically ill when asked to speak publicly in front of a large group, let alone 800 people."

"But that doesn't make sense ... how can you be a top sales performer and not be a social animal?"

"Easy ... these people were top performers because they had the needed strengths that fit the client base, product, and company culture. Think about it ... they go out and meet doctors, provide technical information, and encourage them to prescribe the products to their patients. Trying not to stereotype, but their doctors are most likely technical as well — analytical types with little time for chitchat. The sales people often sit in the waiting room, hoping for just a few minutes with a doctor. Those who don't waste the doctor's time and provide the technical information as quickly and succinctly as possible produce more sales."

"Hmmmmm ..." Jim mumbled in thought, "that is interesting."

Paul and Mario also appeared to be reflecting on their organizations. I interrupted the silence, "Again, putting the right people into the right jobs is part of the equation. Knowing how to reward and drive performance is another part. World-class leaders understand that and do it better than anyone else." You could see the wheels turning in each of their heads — or I was just giving them migraines.

"Let me provide a different example by using golf. Tomorrow Paul is playing in a tournament here at the club. Let's say that he wins the tournament ... not hard to imagine."

"Thanks Sam, I love your confidence in me."

"So, Paul wins and instead of awarding the trophy and having the big dinner tomorrow night, they schedule it for one month from now."

"That is crazy, the energy and excitement of the tournament is long gone." Mario retorted.

"True. Many people, but not all would find that crazy. Now think about how you reward and recognize your people. Someone did something stellar — sold a big client, completed a project on time, came up with an innovative idea. Assuming you want to congratulate or recognize their accomplishment, you should do it immediately. For some, again not all, every minute that passes without a congratulations from you diminishes the value of that recognition. I suspect that if a month passed, Paul could care less about the celebration and might even find it insulting."

"You're probably right. What would be the point? I wouldn't turn down the trophy, but it wouldn't have as much meaning."

"You have to know your people, and you have to adjust your style in order to drive performance. Otherwise, you are just a 'quack' in a leadership position. Effective leaders act as chiropractors, aligning rewards and everything else; people feel better, work better, and produce better results."

Paul reflected, "That includes all levels of the organization ... from the boardroom to the frontline."

"It does indeed."

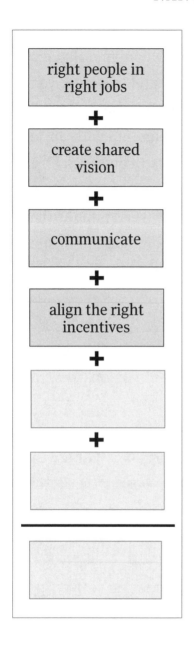

IS CORPORATE SMOKING SOMETHING?

It was 1:30 in the afternoon. Despite five hours of golf and one short break, I was feeling fairly en-

provide the right resources

ergized with only two holes left. My game was amazingly holding together. No major meltdowns in my swing, in Paul's patience, or in anyone's participation in the various leadership exercises. In fact, everyone was surprisingly engaged. So, why not push them a little harder ...

Mario and Jim were analyzing the 17th hole, while Paul churned the ball cleaner posted by the bench next to the cart path.

"How is everyone's energy?" I asked. "Are you ready for another leadership challenge? Or have you had enough?"

With an assortment of "Bring it on," "Don't stop now," and "Show us your best stuff" responses, I continued. "OK, the next element that a leader needs to do is provide the right resources. Maybe a better way to say that is to align, prioritize and allocate the resources appropriately. No company has unlimited resources and unfortunately some employees don't understand that. At the same time, leaders need to be realistic about resources and expectations."

"In our company, resources are very tight. Being the head of IT, we are always being scrutinized. Long gone are the halcyon days when anything we wanted we got, probably because no one understood what we were talking about; then we went through a period of IT fatigue — everyone expected the spend to be completed; now they realize that IT is an ongoing expense and justification for any spend is arduous. The more inspired companies realize that IT is a strategic weapon in their arsenals and invest accordingly."

"Well Mario, let's have a little fun with resources and budgets then. The challenge for this hole is as follows. First, I am the boss."

"Well, we already knew that," Paul chided.

"Thank you. I will be supervising your efforts and keeping track of your resource allocations, which means

I won't be playing this hole. Now I would like to give you a little pep talk. You're a good team and last hole, I mean last year, you did a stellar job. This year we have increased the revenue targets, but unfortunately resources are tighter this year. So I had to make some cuts, but I am sure you can still reach the goal. This hole is a par four, and we only have budget for a total of 10 strokes. How are you feeling so far?"

"Like you are full of crap," Jim confided. "Unfortunately, it is sounding like real life."

"What does that tell you? But no complaining, I want high morale on my team. Plus, I just spent some of our budget on posters that I have placed around the building to encourage you about teamwork, morale, etc. That should inspire you. Anyway, back to the budget. Remember, the three of you combined have to come in on or under budget – only 10 strokes."

Mario interrupted, "You mentioned about budget cuts?"

"Very good Mario, you are definitely one of our high potentials. In fact, in the allocation of resources, you should be fine; although everyone has had to cut. The good news is that we were still able to provide each of you with a golf ball to play the hole. I realize that last year all of you made the goal of par with basically a full set of clubs. But this year is different. This year the re-source allocation will be as follows: In addition to the golf ball that corporate is providing, Jim you are allocat-ed two pieces of golf equipment for this hole; Paul can use three; and Mario has five. Clear?"

Paul confirmed, "So I can use only three pieces of equipment plus the ball? Correct? This shouldn't be too hard. At least I have 50 percent more resources than Jim."

"A little competitive already, ay?" Jim responded.

"Please select your equipment and prepare to tee off."

The 17th hole was a 357-yard dogleg right with no water hazards. Stepping to the tee box, Paul placed the ball on his tee and took a practice swing with his 3 iron. "So you are using your entire equipment budget up-front?" I asked.

"What?" came back the response.

"Well you are using a tee, a 3 iron, and a golf glove — that's three. Oh, I forgot, corporate has offered to be very generous by not counting golf shoes as part of your equipment constraints."

"OK, well, let me take off my glove. How about if I use this tee left from some other foursome?"

"You know that is very resourceful ... maybe Paul should be my high potential."

"Great, now count me as one resource — the 3 iron, OK."

Jim piped up, "Hey, don't break that tee, I plan to use it as well."

With a powerful swing, the ball jettisoned straight down the fairway 175 yards whereupon we lost sight of it. Fortunately for Jim, the tee kicked back remaining in one piece.

Wearing no gloves, Jim stuck the used tee in position and set his ball. He too selected his 3 iron. A strong whack sent it flying down the fairway, landing in an excellent position. Unfortunately for Mario, the tee was shattered and no longer usable.

"No worries, I am certain that I can make my stroke targets and manage my resources. Remember, I am the high potential here." Mario stated proudly. Taking out his driver, Mario hit the ball sending it 220 yards far past Jim's and Paul's. "Gentlemen, take a good look at leadership material."

"This may be the longest hole of the day!" exclaimed Paul, showing his competitive nature.

Jim's second stroke left him 50 yards short of the green. Turning our attention to Paul, we saw why he was irked. Bad news — the reason we had lost sight of his ball was because it rolled into the bunker and was stuck halfway up the forward lip.

"Damn it." Needing the loft to get out of the bunker, Paul decided to use his 9 iron rather than a sand wedge; the 9 iron could come in handy later if he needed to chip onto the green. His strategy worked, he popped out of the bunker and made it another 50 yards closer.

Mario was sitting pretty. His ball was in the middle of the fairway 137 yards from the hole. Using his 7 iron, he easily coasted onto the front of the green.

Forced to play catch up, the nightmare continued for Paul. Staying with his 9 iron, he connected well and sailed the ball another 115 yards, which left him 17 yards short of the green. Another "damn it" could be heard, along with a lament: "I should have made that."

With less than 50 yards left to the hole, Jim gently swung his 3 iron to reach the green. With a large exhale and a broad grin, Jim was pleased. The ball bounced onto the green, barely missing the clover-leaf bunker on the left. "Whew! That was lucky!" exclaimed a relieved Jim. He was on the green in three, leaving him a doable 10-foot putt.

Since Paul was unraveling on this hole, I was starting to reconsider this challenge. While driving to his approach shot, I offered him an out. He was surprisingly good natured about it. "Sam, trust me, I have had a lot more difficult holes than this one. Don't worry. I may not be enjoying my game at this moment, but I am enjoying our discussion and the whole day." With that he grabbed his 9 iron and putter and directed me to take the cart around to the green. I was relieved and did as he requested.

Paul thankfully landed the ball eight feet from the hole. He still had a good chance of making par.

On the green, Mario was contemplating his 20-foot birdie putt. If he missed, "the company" would have no chance of making its 10-stroke goal. Head down and focused, Mario pushed the ball toward the hole. The effort was valiant, but the ball curved to the left and rolled two feet away from the desired destination. Clearly peeved he declared, "I sure as hell read that wrong," completing the hole with a par.

Jim kept eyeing his line; standing over his ball, then retreating to take another look. He finally stepped up and putted. The ball gently running and sliding to within a gopher's breath of the hole. "Unbelievable!" With one last light tap it finally found the hole. "There are days when I hate this game!"

Last up was Paul. Checking his line and analyzing what he just learned from Jim and Mario's experiences, he leaned over the ball and without hesitation lightly knocked the ball. Spinning away from the hole, it began a slow curve and leisurely fell into the hole. "That was close."

Replacing the flagstick, Jim asked, "So how did we do?"

"Well, it was a good team effort, but you missed the goal. We may need to do more cutbacks."

Paul, enjoying a bit of a spar, said, "Given that Jim and I achieved the same goal with a lot less resources, I think you need to reconsider your high potential. I think he is a slacker."

"Boy, they turn on you quickly, don't they," retorted Mario. "I think the goal was totally unrealistic. You said last year we all had full sets of clubs and the goal was 12 strokes for par. 'This year' we made par with significantly fewer resources. I think corporate is smoking something. We were definitely handcuffed. We should be congratulated for achieving what we did!"

"Wow, listen to you. Do you ever hear these kinds of complaints in your company? Or other companies?"

"Sure, all the time. But, like you said, no one has unlimited resources."

"True, Jim. How did you guys feel when Mario got more?"

"That was clearly unfair. It is much easier to be a

high potential when you have more resources. Plus, he never even offered resources to us that he wasn't going to use. He was a miser," Jim teased. "And even with more resources, he did not fare better."

"I think the point is clear, Sam. Resources are another point where the rubber meets the road. If you don't carefully allocate and align them you will create chaos and discord in the system."

"And you have to be realistic. Giving us limited resources and expecting us to make birdies is highly improbable. Challenging us is one thing, but setting us up for failure is unhealthy on so many levels."

"I agree. However, can you think of times when you may have done that?" I challenged. It got very quiet.

"Well, I don't think I have done it to the degree you maybe implying." Mario responded.

"Do you think your people would agree? I am simply proposing that one of the skills leaders need is providing the right resources. When done in combination with all the other factors, communication, etc., people will respond and step up. Your employees want to do a good job and want to reach the goals. Our job as leaders is to provide the culture, environment and resources so that they can succeed."

I continued, "As part of that, leaders must focus on

the vision and allocation of resources to achieve the larger plan. Consequently, allocating more resources to one area because of its strategic importance is absolutely valid. I merely suggest that communicating the reasoning to all reinforces the importance and commitment to the plan as well as expands the understanding and support throughout the team."

"Sam, I hear what you are saying. I bet we do cause a lot of angst in the system by not providing the right resources, misallocating them, or not communicating the reasoning." Paul added.

"Or all of the above," Jim appended.

"Things to think about, huh? And now gentlemen, the much awaited last hole! Yippee."

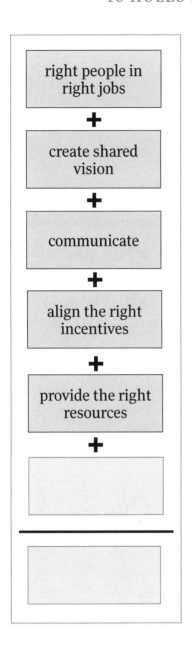

PUT THE PEDAL TO THE METAL

Just to add insult to injury, the final hole was a 481-yard dogleg right par 5. Evidently a very angry masochist had designed the course.

execute, monitor and improve

The foursome playing ahead of us was carting to their third stroke so we were free to tee off. Paul stepped to the tee and hit a beautiful drive. Mario and Jim did the same. I was hopeful that we would finish on a fun golf note after the last hole.

After shifting to the ladies tee box, my entourage wanted to hear the final element. "So did you save the last leadership ingredient for the 18th?" inquired Jim. "Or do we need to play another round of 18 to get the whole thing?"

"Oh, lord no. I'll be lucky to finish this hole; I don't think anyone has the patience to go around with me again!"

Honoring golf etiquette, the three fell silent while I made my final tee stroke of the day. Feeling energized but exhausted, I just wanted to be done. No longer over thinking the stroke or caring much about where it went, I must have relaxed. As soon as I hit the ball, it felt great. That wonderful ping sounded indicating a perfect contact. The ball flew 180 yards down the fairway. It may have been the best drive I ever hit! Picking up the tee and bowing to my gallery, "Thank you. See what some great coaching can do for one's game!"

"That was great," Mario applauded.

"You really have improved today," Jim encouraged.

"Well, we're not done yet," Paul added. Another indication that Frank was right, Paul does take the wind out of your sails. I knew realistically it was going to take a lot more than one round of golf to help Paul.

Ignoring Paul's comment, I moved to the final element, "The last ingredient is execution. Leaders have to execute, monitor and improve the plan. As Joel Barker says, 'Vision without action is merely a dream.' Too many leaders fail to execute. They just don't know how to get things moving. And without having the two buckets of leadership, they frequently can't figure out how to fix 'it.' You can track poor execution to one or multiple elements."

"That's it? Execution?" asked Jim.

"Simple to say, not easy to do. Leaders need to execute, monitor and improve the operations. Their perspective is unique, and if they don't use it appropriately, they put their companies in jeopardy. They need to work ON the system, not IN the system."

"Sam, what do you mean 'not in the system?'" Mario sensing there was more to what I was saying.

"May I suggest we keep moving? Sam can continue to enlighten us as we keep playing," Paul feeling the pressure and continuing to act as our self-appointed time manager.

We jumped into the carts and headed for Mario's and Jim's balls, for once I was closer to the hole than the men. My respectable 180 drive, plus the advantage of the ladies' tee, put my ball in the lead position, at least for the moment.

Watching from the cart, Paul and I relaxed as Mario and Jim took their second strokes. With only one bunker 100 yards from the green, everyone was feeling pretty confident. Chatting between turns including Paul's, I shared with them what I meant by working on the system versus in the system. "Let's imagine two different golf courses with two very different general managers. Manager A is frequently surprised by various course issues — chronic drainage problems, constant equipment breakdowns, regular inventory outages, etc. Consequently, his members regularly complain and his employees are unhappy since they have to deal with cranky members as well as all the problems. Poor manager A is doing the best he can — running from one problem to the next, solving one challenge, only to have five more pop up. Membership is dropping as a result, and manager A must try and promote the club whilst fixing all the problems. His employees respect him because he regularly 'rolls up his sleeves' and gets in and fixes the problem; however, he is always behind and feels as though nothing is stable — as evidenced by the monthly financial reports which are always a surprise since emergency repairs and member losses are difficult to predict.

Mario chuckled, "Sounds as though you have been to my club?"

"You may want to hire manager B then, who is a 'systems thinker.' His club is not without emergencies, but they are infrequent. For example, manager B had a drainage problem when he took over the club. After studying the problem, he identified that the run-off from an adjacent property was the culprit. No additional pumps or re-grading was needed, only a small culvert was required. He solved the root cause and no longer has any drainage issues. He also studied the equipment breakdowns and found that preventative maintenance schedules were not frequent enough. Anyway, you get the picture. And no surprise, the club is doing well, members and employees are happy, and financials are strong. Word of mouth alone ensures a long waiting list for new members — no additional marketing efforts needed there. Yet, just to ensure that his members continue to be happy, he regularly surveys them, questions the board, and meets with them spontaneously in the club.

"Manager B works on the system. If he simply ran from one problem to the next without deep investigation, he would only be working in the system. To improve and lead, you have to work on the system."

"Give me his name and number; I will pass it along to our board president."

Once on the green, I continued the example. "Although manager A is really busy, he is not systemically improving the operation. His employees may be impressed that he grabs a shovel and works with them to fix the immediate drainage problem every time it rains, but he is not fixing the underlying problem. That is what real leaders need to do — improve the system."

After it was my turn to putt, everyone seemed to join in the conversation at once. Jim spoke over the others, "What you are saying is that we need to step back and look at the whole organization and keep improving that?"

"And not get distracted or pulled into the minutia?" Mario added.

"Yes. Now clearly there are times when you do get pulled into the details of a situation; but as leaders, you must also look at the whole system and determine what caused the situation — it may be several steps upstream. Instead many leaders try to track the blame. I suggest to you that ongoing breakdowns IN the system are the fault of leaders not working ON the system. Execution is consequently substandard."

"Well, I have to say Sam, you mixed in a tasty final ingredient," Paul accessed.

"World-class leaders are learners and doers. If someone screws up, they don't play the blame game. Rather they ask questions like did we not have the right resources for the person? Do we have a training issue? Are we communicating clearly and regularly? Do we have hiring issues? They check their two buckets of elements. They look for patterns and trends. They connect the dots so that everyone in the system can execute effectively."

Paul contemplated, "Actually, I can offer another real-life golf example. The tournaments run at this club are executed extremely well, which was not always the case. Our current Event Coordinator (EC) works with his team to plan and execute it. He has got the right people, they know the plan, they have the right resources; I don't know his incentive scheme, but I do know he makes sure the Board knows their names and the great jobs they do. It is rare when a glitch happens; but I dare say, any problems are fixed and not repeated. That is very different from five years ago. The prior EC was a mess. His folks never seemed to know the whole plan, problems arose constantly. The EC would drive his cart from fire to fire. It was embarrassing when we hosted club tournaments here. Now things are calm, you rarely even see the EC on the course during the tournament. As you say Sam, he is gathering information and working ON the system."

Taking a moment, Paul reflected, "I could do a better job working on the system. When a problem arises, my urgency shifts into high gear, and I muscle my people out of the way. I take it over and fix it. Although it makes me feel valued, it may not be the right thing to do. I guess I should rethink my motto, if you want it done right, do it yourself. Doing it right means working *on* the system so we minimize glitches — better still, helping my people to become systems thinkers. Less problems, more golf!"

"We all do that to some extent," Mario consoled Paul. "But Sam is right. If you fix a problem and then just run to the next one, you are not working on the system, you are working in the system."

"Well I recommend we adjourn to the 19th hole and work on our thirst," Jim suggestion was heralded as the best idea of the day. I couldn't have agreed more!

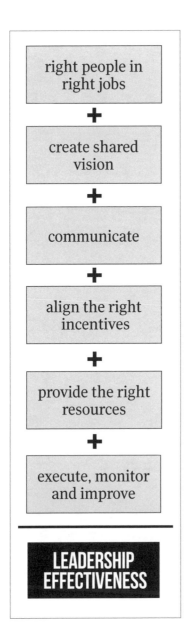

NANCY L. CLARK

THE 19TH HOLE

DRINKS ALL AROUND

Ahhhh ... relief. After almost six hours, there is nothing better than changing out of your golf shoes, washing your hands and face, and collapsing into a comfy chair in the grill. It is the same feeling I get after snow skiing — coming into the lodge from the cold, releasing your feet from those medieval boots, and enjoying a hot chocolate. It is your reward for surviving the day.

I announced to the group, "I am changing the fee, gentlemen. I am buying the first round." Although I never developed much of a taste for beer, I acquiesced to the group. Sitting around the table, snacking on popcorn, and sipping beer, the conversation became more animated. Everyone was having a good time reliving the holes and the comical flubs. At one point, Jim stood up for all to see and demonstrated several of my more graceless strokes.

	1	2	3	4	5	6	7	8	9	Out	
Black Tees	386	207	408	374	404	533	173	384	555	3424	INITIALS
Green Tees	356	182	390	345	374	495	165	349	527	3183	
White Tees	341	170	367	338	324	466	145	313	507	2971	
Men's Par	4	3	4	4	4	5	3	4	5	36	
Handicap	11	15	5	14	7	2	16	12	1		
Paul	4	②	4	4	⑤	⑥	3	⑤	5	38	
Mario	⑤	3	⑤	⑤	4	6	3	⑤	⑥	42	
Jim	⑤	3	⑤	⑤	⑥	6	3	4	⑥	43	
HOLE	**1**	**2**	**3**	**4**	**5**	**6**	**7**	**8**	**9**	**Out**	
Sam	⑦	3	⑤	⑦	⑥	⑧	4	⑥	⑧	54	
Handicap	11	15	5	14	6	2	16	12	1		
Ladies' Par	4	3	4	4	4	5	3	4	5	36	
Red Tees	310	142	345	311	306	449	125	294	453	2735	
Date:						Scorer:					

194

394	365	395	190	521	411	198	388	506	3368	6792	73.8	132	
363	333	352	170	493	386	156	357	481	3091	6274	72.7	128	
330	285	326	141	468	364	132	331	458	2835	5806	70.7	122	
4	4	4	3	5	4	3	4	5	36	72	Rated	Slope	
10	13	9	18	3	6	17	8	4					
8	4	4	3	6	4	2	4	4	39	77			
5	4	5	4	6	3	2	4	5	38	80			
7	5	4	3	6	4	3	4	5	41	84			
10	**11**	**12**	**13**	**14**	**15**	**16**	**17**	**18**	**In**	**Tot**	**Hcp**	**Net**	**Adj**
6	6	5	4	7	6	4	--	6	44	98			
10	13	9	18	3	7	17	8	4					
4	4	4	3	5	4	3	4	5	36	72			
280	264	304	114	447	346	109	312	406	2582	5317	72.0	121	
	Attest:												

Another foursome sitting close by joined in the laughter and expanded the audience for Jim's performance.

As I examined the scorecard, Paul asked, "What's the damage?" I suspected he already knew his score. Jim and Mario passed me their card and I added it onto ours.

"I know that when you get a birdie, you circle it; and, when you get a bogey, you box the score. What do you do when it is a double bogey?" I asked.

"For a double bogey, you double box the score. For an eagle, you double circle it." Mario quickly offered.

"Unfortunately, no double circles on this card. I will create my own identifier for the real ugly scores."

"Ouch. How bad is it? Mario and I agreed not to calculate the final score."

With that, I announced the scores. "For the first time, I broke 100! Thanks to my three coaches."

"Hey, wait a minute. That is only because you didn't play the 17th hole." Jim pointed out.

"Minor details. At least let me bask in the sun for a moment. Next, Jim scored a very respectable 84. Mario was runner up with 80; and, Paul is our champion with 77."

"How did he do that with all those curve balls you threw at us? Let me look at that card." Jim grabbed the card and pretended to check each score closely.

Mario chuckled, "I guess we confirmed today that Paul

is indeed a sandbagger."

"Not true," defended Paul.

Another round was ordered with everyone but Jim opting for a soda this time. Being concerned about drinking and driving, Mario reassured us that he had driven Jim to the club today.

Mario requested a pad of paper from the waitress. Once provided, he then gently pushed it in front me and asked me to write down the leadership elements.

Being the taskmaster that I am, "You know I won't let you off that easily. The three of you tell me what they are and I will write them."

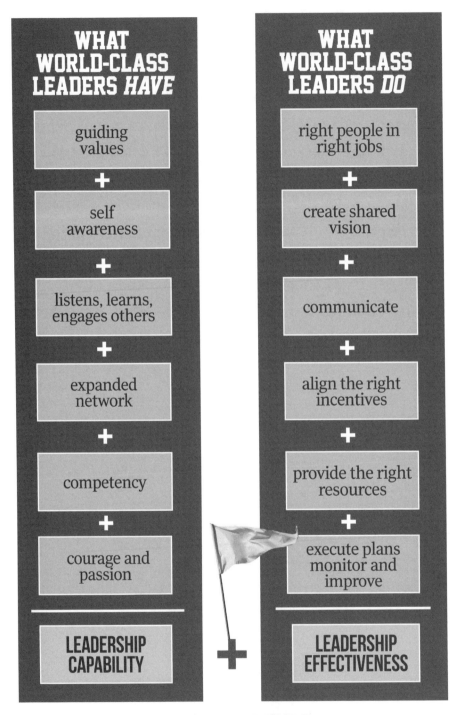

= SUCCESS

My three prize students quickly produced all the elements. When they got stuck they collaborated or relived the hole to help remind them. I am not sure I would have been as astute or accurate. As we reviewed each element, we talked about its application at the various levels of management and leadership. Whether a frontline supervisor or the CEO of a global 100 company, each element was relevant and relative to the level — although perspective, needed strengths, time horizon and work values broaden as you move up the leadership pipeline.

"Let me just underscore the overall purpose. Each organization needs to define what success is. For world-class companies, they understand that with the right leadership they can create a world-class culture; a culture full of engaged and empowered employees. Those engaged employees are the only means to build strong and dedicated customer and supplier relationships. If all those elements are present, those companies are able to maintain and expand a profitable business that is able to attract investors. Remember, check out Chip Conley's book, *Peak*. I think it is a must read for leaders.

"No surprise," Paul added. "Everything is connected and either works together or not. If we don't have capable and effective leaders, we have little or no hope of ever building a strong culture and so on."

Tapping the pad of paper, Jim highlighted, "Leadership is the underlying foundation. You depicted it is an equation of sorts," said Jim. "Yet, it is easy-to-understand. And I agree with the comment earlier — thank you for not 'dumbing' it down. Sometimes consultants try to condense everything into four boxes or whatever. It becomes so broad that it loses any meaning or value."

Mario analyzed the paper, "It does take a lot of elements to be a leader — most you have to have or develop. Maybe there are a few you can leverage from others; but it is clear why we have so few great leaders in business or politics for that matter."

Paul agreed and added, "It is a bit like Earth. To have all the right factors to sustain life is very unique and requires the perfect condition for numerous elements to flourish. No wonder great leaders are also rare. There are multiple elements and conditions that they need to flourish as well. Thankfully, they do not need as many as Earth-like planets, but it does begin to explain why we have a shortage."

"Sam, you haven't touched upon the levels of leadership." Mario probed.

"You're right. That is at least another round of golf. However, just let me say this, depending upon your level your time perspective and work value will change. For example, if you are a frontline supervisor, your time focus may be more day, week and month. If you are a manager of a whole function, your time perspective may be multiple years — in terms of planning, investing and budgeting. If you haven't read the *Leadership Pipeline*, I strongly encourage you to add that to your library as well."

The day ended with all of us promising to play again soon. Mario took the paper with him and asked me to call him on Monday. After handshakes and hugs, Jim and Mario headed to the men's lounge.

Turning to me, Paul continued, "Sam, I am going to have Fran call you on Monday. We need to schedule more time and get my team going as well. I will be back from India week after next, so we can continue then. Plus, if there is anything I can take with me to read on the plane, please email me." Smiling with a little hesitation, "I have to admit I was not sure about this whole coaching thing, and honestly I wasn't looking forward to today; but, and please take this as a compliment, it wasn't bad. I actually enjoyed most of it, even the 10th and 17th holes. You're a good coach, and I look forward to working with you."

"Paul, you are a good coach as well. Between my game and leadership challenges, you exercised amazing patience. Thank you. We still have some work to do, but I am very optimistic."

Driving home I was more than pleased how the day went. It was obvious that Paul and I had gained a greater respect for each other and had reached a deeper working relationship. It was a time to be hopeful.

ONE YEAR AND MANY HOLES LATER

For the first few months after our infamous round of golf, I frequently met with Paul. Attending his staff meetings, observing his interactions, and helping him see and adjust his style when needed. I simultaneously met with Frank. Eventually, bringing the two together and exposing their similarities and differences.

As promised, I introduced some approaches and analytics into the company as well as the "two buckets" to which they are now fondly referred. The most fun was when we took Frank's team offsite for a three-day meeting. The first two days were training. Jaws dropped when both Frank and Paul stood up and shared their strengths and gaps, admitting that they wanted to work more effectively together and requested the help and support of the whole team. From that day forward, the team has worked more effectively together, making progress toward becoming a world-class team.

We continue to cascade the training and tools throughout the company and to help other managers work toward becoming leaders. At a recent meeting with Frank, he noted how different things felt. He was able to spend his energy on strategic issues because the team was working well and was not requiring him to intervene. He confided that, "It just feels healthier and more productive." The employee exodus from Paul has subsided, and he is now a critical support to Frank; no longer a burr in his side.

About once a quarter, I meet with various leaders in the company and check how things are going. We introduced a highly effective leadership program that helps leaders make the transition to each new level; and most importantly, we help leaders become great coaches to their people. Everyone is pleased and results speak for themselves — they are turning around the culture. Decreased turnover, higher productivity, more strategic client and supplier relationships are all positive signs and are flowing to the bottom line.

That is not to say all is perfect. Paul occasionally falls off the leadership wagon and riles Frank; but at least now they have a way to communicate and work through the issue without creating dysfunctional silos.

And much to my delight, Mario and Jim both became clients. Working with Mario on succession planning and career development for his technical people has been both fun and rewarding. We analyzed for Jim the successful profile for his sales team. He is now hiring people who can succeed and thrive in his market. Combined with special sales training, he is delighted at the 22 percent lift in sales, which is particularly rewarding given his competitors are experiencing an opposite trend. Jim has become my best sales person — with all his contacts, he loves sharing how we have helped his team.

With regard to golf, I have tried to play a little more ... maybe averaging once a month whether I need it or not. I have tactfully avoided a "rematch," but I suspect that maybe in the works.

All in all it has been a very good year.

LEADERSHIP SCORECARD

Do you have what it takes? And do you know what to do with it? Take a quick survey of your strengths by using the rating scales below circle the appropriate number from 1 to 5 for each element. Then add up the total to identify your leadership level:

What world-class leaders *have*		
	Assess yourself and circle your score	How you plan to improve ...
Guiding values	Unsure, changing — Clear, unbending 1 2 3 4 5	
Self awareness	Unsure — Clear 1 2 3 4 5	
Listens, learns and engages others	Rarely, if ever — Constantly 1 2 3 4 5	
Expanded network	No/ limited — Massive/ active 1 2 3 4 5	
Competency	Limited in one core discipline — Extensive in multiple core disciplines 1 2 3 4 5	
Courage and passion	Low interest/ avoids personal risk — Infects others/ willing to risk personally 1 2 3 4 5	

Foundation Score = _____

- 30-25 points: You have a strong foundation for leadership; keep it up!
- 24-19 points: You have some work to do; leverage a mentor or coach to help you!
- Less than 19 points: You may have some strong areas, if so work on your "holes." If you are low in most/all the elements, you need to rethink whether you want or enjoy leadership. Find a coach who can help you examine your situation.

What world-class leaders *do*		
	Assess yourself and circle your score	How you plan to improve ...
Right people in right jobs	High turnover Low turnover Low High productivity productivity 1 2 3 4 5	
Create shared vision	Unclear Clear Limited Broad ownership ownership 1 2 3 4 5	
Communicate	Rarely, Constantly Poorly Clearly 1 2 3 4 5	
Align the right incentives	Misaligned Direct alignment 1 2 3 4 5	
Provide the right resources	Unrealistic/ Adequate/ minimal appropriate resources resources 1 2 3 4 5	
Execute plans, monitor and improve	Works IN Works ON the system the system 1 2 3 4 5	

Execution Score = _____

- 30-25 points: You have a strong execution capability for leadership; keep it up!
- 24-19 points: You have some work to do; leverage a mentor or coach to help you!
- Less than 19 points: You may have some strong areas, if so work on your "holes." If you are low in most/all the elements, you need to rethink whether you can execute in a leadership position. Find a coach who can help you examine your situation.

ACKNOWLEDGEMENTS

The process of writing *18 Holes for Leadership* taught me a lot of things, not the least of which is that it takes a village to publish a book. First I would like to thank my client "villagers." My career has been filled with amazing business people from all corners of the Earth. Many have become role models and personal friends — from Terry Burnside at Cardinal Health to Shaun Flanagan at Horizon High Reach to Carol Nitz at Chevron to Tom Kowalski at SI Equipment. These are just a few of the incredible people with whom I have had the pleasure to work.

I have also had the pleasure to learn and work with many colleagues. They were and continue to be teachers, mentors and friends. Many of these relationships started while I was at Arthur Andersen — Michael Doyle, Bob Henry, Bob Hirth, Greg Conlon, Marv Friedman,

Danica Murphy, Jim Walberg, just to name a few. I count myself very fortunate to have such wonderful people in my life.

Another big thank you goes to all those villagers whom I badgered to read and review drafts of the manuscript— Dr. Barry Posner (Co-author, *The Leadership Challenge*, and *Truth About Leadership;* Dean and Professor of Leadership, Santa Clara University), Louie Ehrlich (President and CIO of Chevron Information Technology Company), Nancy Martini (President and CEO of PI Worldwide); Robert Hirth (Executive Vice President, Protiviti, Inc.); Stephen Drotter (Co-author, *The Leadership Pipeline*); Danica Murphy (Co-author, *Introduction to Type and Conflict*); Peg Kingman (author, *Not Yet Drown'd* and *Original Sins*); and, Rob McWilliams (President, Robert McWilliams Productions, Inc.). Their comments, reviews and testimonials were and are greatly appreciated.

A new subdivision of the village now includes 3L Publishing. Michele Smith for her persistence in staying in touch and believing in *18 Holes*; Michelle Gamble-Risley for her patience and masterful editing capabilities; Erin Pace for her magical graphic talents; and the whole 3L team that keeps the drum beating and the process moving. They have guided me through this new world of publishing with patience and support.

In particular, I would like to thank my immediate villager — my husband, Del. His patience and support are unwavering. I am truly blessed to be able to share my life with someone who is my greatest cheerleader, therapist and friend.

And lastly, I want to thank my father to whom the book is dedicated. He definitely was the chief of our village and taught me and my sister many lessons. He touched so many people and still to this day they reflect on the positive impact he had on their lives. Dad, you are missed. But maybe *18 Holes* can continue to share the lessons you taught me.

SUGGESTED READING

Golf:

Sorry, you are on your own. If you have suggestions, please send them to me! I could use them.

Organization and Leadership:

Here is a list of some of my favorites:

- *The Democratic Corporation*, Russell L. Ackoff
- *Future Edge*, Joel Arthur Barker
- *Execution, The Discipline of Getting Things Done*, Larry Bossidy & Ram Charan
- *First, Break All the Rules*, Marcus Buckingham & Curt Coffman
- *The Leadership Pipeline*, Ram Charan, Stephen Drotter, and James Noel
- *Peak: How Great Companies Get Their Mojo from*

Maslow, Chip Conley and Tony Hsieh
- *Built to Last,* James C. Collins and Jerry I. Porras
- *Good to Great,* Jim Collins
- *Quality is Free,* Philip B. Crosby
- *How to Make Meetings Work,* Michael Doyle and David Straus
- *Out of the Crisis,* W. Edwards Deming
- *Management Challenges for the 21st Century,* Peter F. Drucker
- *The Change Monster,* Jeanie Daniel Duck
- *Man's Search for Meaning,* Viktor E. Frankl
- *Outliers, The Tipping Point,* Malcolm Gladwell
- *It's Not Luck, The Goal,* Eliyahu M. Goldratt and Jeff Cox
- *What Got You Here, Won't Get You There,* Marshall Goldsmith
- *Emotional Intelligence,* Daniel Goleman
- *Beyond Certainty, The Age of Paradox, The Age of Unreason,* Charles Handy
- *Synchronicity,* Joseph Jaworski
- *The Leadership Challenge,* James M. Kouzes & Barry Z. Posner
- *The Five Dysfunctions of a Team, The Five Temptations of a CEO,* Patrick Lencioni
- *The Fifth Discipline,* Peter M. Senge
- *The Team Handbook,* Peter R. Scholtes
- *Leadership and the New Science,* Margaret J. Wheatley

ABOUT THE AUTHOR

Nancy Clark is president of Leadership Dynamics, Inc., a global management consulting firm specializing in leadership development, strategic planning and resource alignment, team and sales performance improvement. Her mission has always been to help organizations become healthy, profitable, and great places for people to do great work.

As a consultant and keynote speaker, Nancy has worked with thousands of leaders and executive teams in organizations ranging from Global 100 to family-owned to nonprofit. She has delivered hundreds of keynote addresses and workshops on leadership, organizational change, teamwork and corporate culture. Her book, *18 Holes for Leadership*, released Fall 2010, addresses the questions: Do have what it takes to be a leader? And, do you know what to do with it?

Previously, Nancy led a management consulting practice at Arthur Andersen where she worked with many of the Fortune 500 companies. Growing up in a family business, she developed an early understanding of leadership and the complexities of management which allow her to span and understand the issues of small to large organizations.

She is also dedicated to helping public education and developing youth leaders. She led the West Coast (USA) effort of the School of the Future Project for Arthur Andersen which co-developed with Alameda Unified School District a state-of-the-art, project based, teacher-facilitated program. From 1990-2000, she served as board president of Alternatives in Action, a non-profit that creates youth-led charter schools/educational environments; and, from 2000 to the present, she serves as board president of On the Move, a non-profit that is dedicated to supporting disadvantaged youth and their communities.

Nancy lives in the San Francisco Bay Area with her husband, Del, their two horses, Mr. B and Tessie, and their two dogs, George and Gracie. You can reach Nancy through Leadership Dynamics, Inc. website: www.leaders-inc.com.